CENTERED

A BEGINNER'S GUIDE TO POTTERY WHEEL AND CERAMIC TECHNIQUES

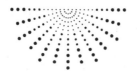

KENDYL ARDEN

Centered

A Beginner's Guide to Wheel-thrown Pottery and Ceramic Techniques

Kendyl Arden

result of the use of the information contained within this document, including, but not limited to, errors, omissions, or inaccuracies.

CONTENTS

INTRODUCTION

"He who works with his hands is a laborer. He who works with his hands and his head is a craftsman. He who works with his hands and his head and his heart is an artist."

— *ST. FRANCIS OF ASSISI*

The art of turning clay into functional ceramics is the oldest of humankind's handicrafts; pottery has been used in the course of daily human activity since the earliest times. Pots in varying degrees of fragmentation are one of the most common finds uncovered by archaeologists. Clay has been used since prehistoric times to make both functional items, and works of three-dimensional art.

The words 'pottery' and 'pot' are derived from the old English, *potian*, meaning to push, which refers to the process of throwing clay on the wheel. The term 'pot' is used to refer to any number of forms made of clay. Considering that the pottery wheel is a tool that only does one thing—i.e., spins in a circle—wheel throwing offers an astounding number of possible techniques and results.

Many people are drawn to pottery-making because it provides a unique means of self-expression in sculptural form, when words are not the right medium for expressing what feels inexpressible. Connecting to this ancient craft in times of stress or distress is a calming escape, and taps into the transformative and healing potential of artistic creation. For some people, throwing clay on the wheel can become quite addictive!

The tactile experience of working with a natural medium that responds readily to direction by your own hands is highly therapeutic. When both body and mind are fully engaged in the repetitive motions of spinning and shaping clay, outside distractions fall away, and the process becomes a vehicle for entering a flow state. There are so many times where students will say to me, "This is so therapeutic!", "I completely lost track of time!", or "I feel so calm after I throw.". This is likely because wheel throwing is the perfect activity to get into a "flow state".

FLOW: CREATIVITY AS LIFE'S OPTIMAL EXPERIENCE

Being in flow is defined as being in an optimal state, where we both feel and perform at our best. In this state, we are fully present and completely absorbed in a task. You've probably heard some people refer to this state as being "in the zone."

This gives us the sense of having stepped away from our everyday routines into a different reality, where our action and awareness merge, attention is effortless, and we experience immediate feedback from the process we are engaged in (Doyle, 2017).

In a flow state, our brain waves move from fast moving beta waves of normal waking consciousness, to the slower alpha states associated with daydreaming, and theta states usually achieved during REM sleep, or in the hypnagogic state before we fall asleep. The part of the brain responsible for self-judgment quiets down, silencing our inner critic, and enhancing our ability to imagine new possibilities (Kotler, 2014).

These changes in the brain cause positive physiological changes as well; a 2010 study on classical pianists showed that musicians in a flow state experienced deeper breathing and a slower heart rate (Robb, 2019).

During flow states, the brain also releases the performance-enhancing chemicals dopamine, endorphins, anandamide, and serotonin. These further boost focus and creativity, and increase pattern-cognition and the ability to combine ideas together in new ways. A Harvard study on flow concluded that being in flow doesn't only increase creativity in the moment, it trains the brain to be more creative over the long term as well (Kotler, 2014).

Giovanni Moneta, an academic psychologist at London Metropolitan University, and the author of *Positive Psychology: A Critical Introduction*, notes that getting into flow is easier when we are engaging in activities that are meaningful to us, that we find challenging, and for which we feel that we have the required skills (Robb, 2019). Ultimately, those who regularly experience flow states report improved overall life satisfaction, well-being, and feelings of happiness. Finding activities to enter into flow state is just one reason to begin your own pottery practice!

Working with clay to create functional and artistic pieces of pottery offers the means to discover new avenues for creativity, healing, and self-actualization. As you develop your technical skills and unique style, you may discover hidden strengths and expressive abilities. This can lead to greater optimism, confidence, and a sense of purpose and accomplishment.

SO WHY PICK UP POTTERY?

There are plenty of good reasons why pottery-making is as popular as ever, and continues to draw new students eager to learn.

- **It's a fantastic creative outlet.** Pottery-making allows for virtually unlimited exploration, experimentation, and expression.
- **It improves flow, spontaneity, and mood.** By allowing yourself to be completely absorbed in the creative process, your mind and body begin to work together in perfect synergy. In a flow state, concentration becomes so focused that everything else falls away. Being in this optimal state of consciousness heightens all aspects of performance, including creativity.
- **It's a great stress-buster!** Using our hands to create something is a natural inclination. Our sense of touch is seated in our hands, and the focus required to make pottery encourages outside worries to take a backseat.
- **It helps you reconnect with your emotional center.** Working with a pottery wheel requires centering the clay on the wheel, and preventing it from spinning out of shape. Focusing on this process also helps to center your emotional state.
- **It's grounding!** Being made from earth, clay has a natural vibration and calming energy.
- **Your creations might last thousands of years!** The pottery objects you make today could be the archeological finds of future generations!

While all of this sounds wonderful, you may be

wondering where to begin. There seems to be a lot to learn. What about all the tools? Where does one even start?

While pottery-making does require some preparation, and a few basic tools to start, the good news is that there are various options available to meet your specific situation. Perhaps you're not quite ready to set up your own studio, but would like to begin learning a few basics to practice in a rented or communal space. You might not be ready to invest in a pottery wheel, but have access to one you can use. Either way, by the end of this book you'll be equipped with all the basic knowledge you need to get started with the basics of throwing on the wheel. I will show you how you can create functional art out of clay, and you'll learn a valuable new skill along the way! We'll be covering:

- How to set up and maintain your studio
- What kind of clay to choose, and the materials and tools you need to get started
- How to throw a form on the potter's wheel from start to finish
- Different forms and techniques you can use when throwing, bowls, handles, tea pots, vases, pitchers, plates, or jars

My name is Kendyl Arden, and I am an artist, fine art teacher, and art therapist living and working in Chicago, Illinois. I am the founder of a pottery studio called Muze Inc., where I teach local residents how to throw on the potter's wheel.

My work has been exhibited at a variety of art festivals and solo exhibition shows focusing on clay as the predominant medium. I have taught art classes throughout America, and taught pottery classes when living overseas in Kathmandu, Nepal.

My deep passion for pottery, and extensive experience in both studying and teaching pottery, inspired a desire to share this knowledge in an easily accessible way. Alongside this, I also use the arts to help individuals heal, through art therapy groups that I lead.

Helping you successfully create beautiful pottery on the potter's wheel matters deeply to me, because I have seen how art-making can be a source of healing and respite from the stressors of life. What you're about to learn is my condensed knowledge from years of experience, which has helped me to throw beautiful vessels of all shapes and sizes on the potter's wheel, and go on to become a successful artist and teacher for students around the globe.

To begin with, we'll look at the basic tools and equipment you will need to start making pottery, and the methods and reasons for keeping your studio clean.

BASIC STUDIO TOOLS, AND THE IMPORTANCE OF STUDIO UPKEEP

BASIC POTTERY TOOLS

There are two primary methods of working with clay; building by hand or throwing on a potter's wheel. Both disciplines make use of some basic pottery tools; while clay can be molded, shaped, and smoothed by your hands alone, the use of some tools takes your pottery to a new dimension in terms of possibilities. Having some basic tools also makes working with clay easier, and elevates the final look of your creations.

Not all tools are absolutely necessary to begin with. A beginners set of essential tools will usually include basics like a needle tool, potter's rib, wire-cutting tool, sponges, and a trimming loop.

- **Needle Tool:** These long, heavy needles—usually set into wooden, plastic, or metal handles—are one of the most versatile tools in pottery. They can be used for trimming the edges of pieces while they're still on the wheel, or for scoring slabs and coils during hand-building.

- **Water bucket:** a 2 gallon bucket will be necessary to have on your wheel whenever you are throwing. This will hold water and any discarded clay scraps from your vessel.

- **Sponges:** Sponges are one of the most useful tools to have in your toolbox, and will be used to absorb or distribute water during throwing; for smoothing out the surface of clay; and for cleaning up your workspace. You will want large sponges for cleaning, as well as a small round hand sponge to help apply water to your vessels during the throwing process.

- **Wire Clay Cutter:** Also known as the wire cut-off tool, this is a traditional tool consisting of stainless steel wire attached to hardwood handles. Wire cutters are used for cutting and slicing lumps of clay, and for cutting pots off the wheel. Very flexible wire or fishing line work best when throwing off the mound.

- **Ribbon and Loop Tools**: These are handy for trimming greenware (clay pieces that have been shaped but not yet fired), especially the feet of pots; for adding texture and definition; and for hollowing out handmade pieces.

- **Ribs and Metal Scrapers:** These are used to help shape and smooth pots as they are being formed on the wheel. They're also used during the rib-and-hand method of making coiled pots. Ribs come in different shapes and sizes, and can be made of wood, rubber, plastic, or metal. Scrapers are similar to ribs, but are lighter, and are usually made of steel, rubber, or wood. They're used to smooth wet and soft leather hard greenware. Ribs and scrapers are, overall, used to give a smooth finish.

- **Modeling Tool:** These come in a variety of shapes and sizes, with the triangular-headed varieties being ideal for trimming pieces while throwing on the wheel. A wooden modeling tool is often used for removing excess clay from the base of a vessel.

- **Calipers:** used to accurately measure the inside and outside lid-to-pot ratio. Calipers are needed to measure lids for jars, and to match the base of a

cup to the center of a saucer, or the base of a
pitcher to the floor of a basin.

- **Rolling Pin:** for rolling out slabs of clay to an even
  thickness.

- **Clay Cutters:** available in various shapes and sizes,
  these are used to carve shapes into slabs of clay.

- **Glazes and Stains**: You'll use these to add color to
  your ceramics, either as an underglaze, or added to
  the last coat of finish.

- **Glaze Brush**: for applying stains, glazes, washes or
  wax; a glaze brush leaves a smooth finish. The best
  brushes are made of sumi or bamboo; these can
  hold a lot of fluid, and still have a pointed end.

Since many tools are fairly small and easy to misplace, it's
best to keep them in a box where they'll be organized and
accessible. You could use a heavy-duty plastic artist or tackle
box for this, and a utensil tray to hold small hand-building
tools.

Additional equipment you should have includes towels
and an apron and chamois cloth. Keep some old absorbent
towels at hand, and one across your knees, as these are ideal
for rough cleaning your hands. Since pottery can be rather

messy, it's a good idea to wear a bib-type apron to protect your clothes.

Chamois is perfect for compressing and smoothing the upper edges of thrown pieces, and to smooth leather hard pieces. Dampen slightly before use, and be sure to wash properly after every session.

You will also want a variety of plastic buckets and storage containers, plastic bags, and/or rolls of thick plastic wrap.

CHOOSING THE RIGHT POTTERY WHEEL

A pottery wheel is an investment you'll need to make if you intend to start making wheel-thrown pottery. The cost of this depends on its capabilities and features. When buying your first pottery wheel, you may feel that you should buy a pottery wheel suitable for beginners. Before deciding on a model, consider your long-term goals as well, taking into account the features you want right now as well as those you think you'll want in five years from now. If kept properly maintained, an electric wheel can last ten years or more, while a kick wheel can last a lifetime.

A kick wheel pottery wheel is manually operated, and works by the foot power the potter supplies to keep the wheel moving. Kicking the flywheel with your foot closer to the center increases the speed of the wheel in a smooth rhythm, and the momentum will last for several minutes. Kick wheel pottery wheels can be tiring to use for longer periods, and can be hard on the knees. Kicking near the edge requires more effort and is more tiring.

Kick wheel pottery wheels are also generally quite heavy, and difficult to transport and move around. In addition, they're quite loud, so you need to decide if the noise they make will be an issue for you. Electric wheels, operated by electronic controls, are much smaller and lighter, and therefore more portable.

Key features you'll want to look out for are a wheelhead of 8 to 14 inches, ¼ to 1 HP, removable basins and bat pins, adjustable speeds and direction, and loudness of the wheel.

Well-known brands of electric pottery wheels include Brent, Lockerbie, Shimpo, and Speedball. Brent wheels have been manufactured in the US since 1969, and are recognizable by their bright yellow color. Shimpo offers some of the quietest wheels available on the market, with popular models being the VL Whisper and the RK Whisper. Speedball wheels offer high quality performance and good value, and the Artista Portable is a cost-effective beginner model that can handle up to 25 pounds of clay.

Budget electric models (around $500) will have more basic capabilities, a smaller clay load capacity, and less power and speed. They'll also be less durable.

For standard models, the cost will be closer to $1000. These will have larger wheel heads and more power, as they're more likely to have an industrial motor. Their operation will be smoother, and they'll also be more durable.

Their clay load is likely to be between 150 and 250 pounds of clay.

Additional features could include a reversing plug to change wheel head direction, and a two-part splash pan. The latter is a molded plastic tray that fits around the wheel, which keeps clay and water from spraying all over you, the floor, and surrounding areas. While a splash pan helps to keep things clean, some artists find them to interfere with the throwing process.

Many, but not all, electric wheels have a forward and reverse switch to allow for spinning in either direction. Which direction the wheel should be spinning depends on a few factors. If you are right-handed, you will most likely find it most comfortable to spin the wheel counter-clockwise, whereas left-handed people usually prefer the clockwise direction.

You might also want to change the direction depending on the process you are busy with. You might find it more comfortable to use counter-clockwise for some tasks, and clockwise for others. For example, some right-handed potters will use counter-clockwise for throwing, but clockwise for trimming. Be sure to check the direction that the wheel turns before buying.

A professional wheel will set you back over $1000, but will run extremely quietly and smoothly. Features it will typically have include more power, smoother foot pedal control, a reversible electronic speed control, a cooling fan, and a built-in splash pan. The clay load is likely to be between 400 and 450 pounds.

You'll need to decide if portability is a feature that's important to you. While portable wheels are smaller and lighter, they generally have a smaller clay load capacity. They're commonly used by teachers, and for giving demonstrations at events and arts festivals.

The size of the wheelhead is another factor to consider. This is the revolving piece mounted in the center of the pottery wheel, where clay pieces will be formed during the throwing process. Most are round and flat metal surfaces ranging from 8" to 14" in diameter. A larger wheelhead allows you to throw large pots, platters, and other pieces with wide bases.

Pottery wheel bats are thin disks made of plaster, wood, or plastic that are fixed to the wheel head with pins. These are used when making a piece that could be difficult to lift off the wheel head. Wheel bats need to fit the dimensions of the wheelhead, as the configuration of pins, their number, and distance from the center of the wheelhead can vary.

Having a wheel with built-in bat pins allows you to use different-sized bats. To enable this, make sure the model you buy has bat pins that can be removed easily.

HOW TO MAKE A PLASTER SLAB FOR RECLAIMING AND DRYING CLAY

Having a plaster slab is very useful for hardening up reclaimed clay as it will speed up the drying process. When working on a plaster slab, you need to take great care not to get plaster fragments into the clay, as this will cause cracks and surface pops during firing. Make a habit of wiping the slab down regularly, and handle it with care.

You can make a plaster slab yourself using plaster mix and water; this will give you a sturdy slab that will last a long time. Adding some herculite plaster to the mix adds strength, and helps to prevent flakes from chipping off. Making the slab quite thick helps to draw the moisture out of clay faster, and prevents the board from getting saturated with water.

An easy way to do this is to use a plastic storage container, mix it up in there, and let it dry. You could also make plaster slabs using some 9 x 12 inch foil cake pans, or a shallow box, such as a clean pizza box. You'll need some pottery plaster, a scale, and some buckets. Calculate the size of the container in cubic inches by measuring all the dimensions. Divide this number by 80; this will give you the amount in quarts of water you will need.

Multiply that number by three to give you the number in pounds of plaster that you need. If you are using herculite plaster as well, add that in a 1:3 ratio of herculite to pottery plaster.

Pour the water into the container, and then slake in the

plaster to the water gradually. Add handfuls at a time—don't dump it all in at once! Let the plaster soak for a few minutes, bouncing the container occasionally to get any air bubbles out. Then, mix the plaster thoroughly with your hands for a few minutes (making sure your hands are clean). Bounce the container a few more times to get any remaining bubbles out.

Allow to dry for three or four days. When the slab is dry, upend the container over a piece of thick foam, and gently tap the container with a hammer until the slab falls out. There's no need to line the container with anything, as the slab will shrink slightly as it dries, and then detach from the container.

WEDGING BOARDS AND TABLES

A wedging table or board is an essential tool that should be in every potter's studio. This is where you will wedge your clay before throwing it on the wheel, which basically means removing any trapped air in the clay, and ensuring it has a uniform consistency throughout.

Depending on your budget, you can buy these ready-made, or you can make your own from either plaster or plywood covered in canvas. Working on canvas is recommended, as it protects your table, and stops the clay from sticking. Tables can also be made of concrete, Masonite, concrete board, or hardibacker board. Natural stone and cement boards are additional options—these are durable, non-absorbent, and won't stick to the clay as much as canvas.

Using a portable wedging board allows you to wedge your clay outside if you wish, and also stores away easily.

The position of your wedging table or board should be relatively low, so that when you are standing upright you should be able to place your fingers on the table with your elbows slightly bent. This is important to safeguard the long-term health of your wrists.

SETTING UP YOUR POTTERY STUDIO

In setting up your studio space, there are a few important factors you'll need to consider. Firstly, define your level of interest. Are you planning to start small and work your way up to a larger, dedicated space, or are you going all in from the start?

Establish the size of the space you have available, or are willing to create, to house your studio. Consider the space you have available. Do you have a spare bedroom or porch you could enclose? Perhaps you have an outbuilding or garage you could convert, or you might even want to build a freestanding studio. If you're not ready to build your own studio, you might want to look at renting studio space to begin with.

If you plan on doing mostly handbuilding, you'll need far

less space, as you could just build on your kitchen table. Wheel-throwing is messier, and a pottery wheel takes up a fair bit of space. Good lighting in your studio is essential, and ambient lighting is preferable to spotlights.

You'll need some storage space to keep your clay, materials, tools, glazes etc. You'll also need some shelving for your completed greenware. It's very important to have a place for clay objects to dry slowly, where they won't be bumped or jostled. The drying process is critical for greenware, since it can't be fired until it's bone dry; otherwise it can deform or break in the kiln. Greenware is also extremely fragile when bone dry. You'll need enough space for both greenware and bisqueware. Bisque is pottery that has undergone initial firing, but still needs glaze firing.

Consider whether you plan to install your own kiln, or plan to rent kiln space. Most electric kilns need heavy-duty electrical wiring, which will have to be installed by a professional. If you plan to use a kiln in an enclosed space, you will need to have a proper ventilation system installed. Ventilation is essential, as gases from clay bodies and glazes are released during firing.

Ventilation is also important if you will be mixing your own clay bodies and glazes, or using an airbrush. Mixing should be done outside, or in a room with its own ventilation system. Airbrushes should only be used in a vented spray booth, and you should wear an appropriate respirator.

Access to water for working with clay, and cleaning up afterwards, is essential. Avoid letting clay go down the drain, as it will eventually clog up your plumbing. Glazes may contain chemicals hazardous to the environment, and that can be difficult for sewage systems to filter out. It's advisable to use a series of buckets, for rinsing your hands and tools, before washing your hands in the sink.

THE IMPORTANCE OF KEEPING YOUR STUDIO CLEAN

Dust is an unavoidable part of working with clay, but allowing clay dust to accumulate can cause long-term health issues. Clay dust contains silica micro-particles, which can hang in the air for a long time. Powdered glazes contain alumina, which can also go airborne. Clay and glaze dust can be harmful to your lungs; when inhaled over an extended period of time, silica can cause a serious lung ailment called silicosis.

High-temperature clays, such as porcelain and stoneware, can contain up to 30% silica, while low-fire clays have much lower proportions.

It's essential to take the necessary precautions to ensure you have a safe working environment. The best way to minimize dust buildup is to clean your studio space regularly with clean water. This prevents dust from being airborne, and subsequently inhaled.

Keep a spray bottle handy, as this can help immensely to keep dust under control. Wipe up dust when you see it to prevent it from spreading to other areas of your studio, or into your house through the ventilation system. Mop the floor daily, or hose down if you have a floor drain. Be sure to keep your pottery clothes separate from the rest, and wash them separately.

Clean down your wheel and work table with a wet sponge, and put all trimmings in a reclaim bucket. This is preferable to removing bone-dry trimmings, which can stir up dust when they break up. Hardened clay can also be placed in your reclaim bucket, and it will break down into a slurry over time.

Before wedging on a canvas table, it's a good idea to wipe it down with a damp cloth or sponge first, to prevent stirring up dust.

Mixing up clay from a dry mix creates a lot of dust, so it's better to mix outside if you don't have a good ventilation system. Be sure to wear a proper dust mask with a snug fit when mixing clay, glazes, or sanding greenware or bisque-ware. It should be NIOSH-rated for fine particles, so that it traps the silica. If you suffer from allergies, or are sensitive to dust, it's essential to wear a respirator.

Avoid dusting, sweeping, or vacuuming in the studio as these methods stir up dust in the air. If you use a rug to prevent tracking of clay to other areas, use an outdoor carpet that can be hosed down.

You might want to create a simple checklist for cleaning, and put this up somewhere you can see it. When you are working with a lot of different tools, it can be easy to overlook something.

Every studio is different, so you can tailor your checklist to suit your studio and work habits. A typical checklist might look something like the following:

- Clean debris and clay scraps from the wheel and work table, and place these in your reclaim bucket.

- Wipe down your tools, tool-box, and wheel with a sponge.

- Clean up debris from the floor, and place usable scraps in reclaim buckets.

- Mop up dust or slip from the floor.

- Clean debris from around the sink, and wipe down with a sponge.

- Wash sponges and towels, and hang or place where they will dry easily.

2

DECIDING HOW MUCH CLAY TO USE

Before you even get on the wheel, you will need to decide how much clay to use when throwing carious forms. Throwing weight will be impacted by different variables, these should be taken into consideration when prepping your clay.

VARIABLES THAT AFFECT CLAY WEIGHT

- **Wall Thickness Affects Throwing Weight:** The wall thickness will impact how much clay you will need to use, and this changes with each potter. Everyone is different and has a different preference for throwing thicker or thinner walls. Thicker walls will feel sturdy and heavy and require more clay, while thinner walls will become light and delicate, thus needing less clay for the same form.

- **Pot Profile:** How the pot is shaped is another variable to consider. Depending on the shoe of the form, you may nee more or less clay. For example, a mug with a narrow base will need less clay on the bottom, whereas a mug with a wide base will need to have more clay left behind. Again, this is up to each potter's preference.

- **Foot height:** Similarly, if you want to have a thick foot on the bottom to trim, you will need to leave the base thicker than if you didn't want to do much trimming. The more trimming you want to do, the thicker you will need to leave your piece.

- **Adding Designs to the Basic Pot:** Adding design elements on to your pottery can also impact how much clay to use. If you are planning on carving into the form you will need to leave the form thicker to have more clay to work with so that you do not poke through the piece. This will add to the clay weight that you start with.

- **Clay body:** Each clay type that you use will vary in shrinkage rate. The shrinkage rate will need to be taken into consideration when you are throwing

on the wheel. For example, if a clay has a 10%
shrinkage rate, you will want to make the form
10% larger than what is expected. Using clays with
a larger shrinkage rate means increasing the
throwing weight.

These variables show that each potter will throw with a
different amount. You can look at different clay charts, but
everyone is different and what works for one potter may not
work for another. So, if there are so many variables to
consider, how can one decide how much clay to use?

DECIDING HOW MUCH CLAY YOU NEED

Clay weight charts will give a good starting point and will
show you the average weight to use. Although this is typically the case, you do not need to utilize exactly what a chart
states and it is beneficial to make adjustments as you go
depending on what your personal preferences and throwing
styles are. In the beginning of your throwing journey you
will use much more clay than you will later on. This is very
normal.

With time, your walls will become more consistent and
likely thinner, so you will loose less clay as your progress. It
is also important to note that if you start throwing with too
much clay you will face a lot of challenges as it will require
more strength and technique, and it will be very hard to
learn the fundamentals. A good rule of thumb is to begin by

throwing a ball of clay that is no larger than the circumference of your hand, but as you progress in skill you will likely be able to throw larger and heavier pieces.

Pottery Weight Chart

ITEM	SIZE (H X W)	WEIGHT
• Standard Mug	5 x 3 in	12 oz, 350 g
• Large Mug/Stein	7 x 4 in	1.23-1.5 lbs, 550-700 g
• Tall Tumbler/ Pint Glass	6 x 3 in	1- 1.25 lbs, 450-550 g
• Small Bowl (condiments)	2 x 4 in	6-8oz, 150-225 g
• Medium Bowl (Cereal, Soup)	3 x 5 in	1.25-1.5 lbs, 550-700 g
• Large Bowl (serving, Mixing)	4 x 10 in	4-6lbs, 1.8-2.7 kg
• Small Plate (Salad, Dessert)	1 x 7 in	2 lbs, 900 g
• Dinner Plate	1.5 x 10 in	4-5 lbs. 1.8-2.3 kg
• Large Plate/ Platter	2 x 14 in	6-8 lbs, 2.7-3.6 kg
• Small Pitcher	5 x 3 in	1 lb- 450 g
• Large Pitcher	12 x 5 in	4 lbs, 1.8 kg
• Tea Pot	7 x 7 in	4-5 lbs, 1.8-2.3 kg
○ Lid		6-8 oz, 150-225 g
○ Spout		6-8 oz, 150- 225 g

Here is a general throwing weight chart for specific forms. Adjust the chart as you go, and make changes in alignment with your skill level and preferences.

3

CLAY BODIES, CLAY STATES, AND HOW TO AVOID S-CRACKS

CLAY BODIES

All clay types contain alumina and silica in different ratios. Silica forms the central structure of clay, and is the glass-forming component in both clay and in glazes. Alumina has a high melting point, and provides mechanical strength to the clay.

The chemical composition of clay is one molecule of alumina, and two molecules of silica, bonded with two molecules of water. When clay is heated to high temperatures, the bonded water loosens and escapes, gases and bonded water are released, and the silica melts a little. The bonds between the clay particles become very strong.

CHOOSING THE RIGHT CLAY TYPE

In choosing which clay to work with, there are quite a few variables to consider. These include the kind of end product you have in mind, your skill levels, and the type of kiln you will be using when firing your pottery.

For throwing on the wheel, your clay needs to have high plasticity to make it workable on the wheel. Plasticity refers to how flexible the clay is, and is determined by the size of the particles, the clay's water content, and age.

It also needs strength to be able to stand upright when throwing taller forms. Bear in mind that higher plasticity means the clay will shrink faster, and has greater potential for warping during the drying process.

For beginners, it's best to choose a clay that has a relatively lower rate of water absorption, since the longer clay is worked on the wheel, the softer it becomes as water gets mixed in.

Hand-building with clay requires both strength and plasticity to allow the piece to hold its form as it is constructed and handled, without sagging or cracking. This is especially true for larger or flatter pieces. Plasticity is also important when building extreme shapes such as sharp angles, or during coiling.

CLAY TYPES

Earthenware Clays: These are the oldest known clay types, and are the most common kind found naturally. They have high plasticity, and are easy to work with, and are therefore good for both hand-building and wheel-throwing. These clays contain iron and other mineral impurities, which causes them to reach their optimum hardness at lower temperatures.

Fired earthenware (commonly called terracotta) yields an unvitrified ceramic that is typically red or orange due to the iron oxide content. These colors appear more vivid due to firing at low temperatures. Unglazed earthenware is porous, and is not suitable for vessels that hold liquids.

Glazed earthenware is more fragile, and chips more easily than glazed stoneware, and is therefore usually made thicker.

Stoneware Clay: Popular for use in dinnerware and mugs, stoneware is more durable and chip-resistant than earthenware. While stoneware is a lower quality clay than porcelain, it's more durable and good value for money. This is a good clay for beginners, who often need to work their clay a bit longer than more seasoned potters.

Porcelain or Kaolin Clays: These are the best clays for pottery, but are usually more expensive. They yield finely textured pottery that is white or pale in color. Kaolin clays absorb water quite quickly, and have a lower natural plasticity, so they can be a bit more challenging for beginners to work with. Due to their high silicate content, porcelain clays are fired at higher temperatures. Porcelain pottery is impermeable to water without glazing, while stoneware and earthenware are not.

Ball Clays: These are white or nearly white ceramic clays with high plasticity, sourced primarily from deposits in Devon and Dorset, UK. These English clays are composed of very fine particles, and contain a large amount of the mineral kaolinite. The fine texture means that it absorbs water readily, and this gives it exceptional plasticity. Ball clay derives its name from the way in which it quickly turns into a ball after being handled, having been cut from the floor of a pit in cubes. The word 'clay' is in fact derived from the old English 'claeg,' meaning sticky.

These clays have been used in the making of fine ceramics since the days of well-known 18th-century potters such as Josiah Wedgewood, Astbury, and Spode, and are rather rare these days. They are normally sold in powdered form, and added to other clay types to enhance performance. Ball clay can be added to porcelain clay to make it easier to shape.

Some potters prefer to buy clay in dry form, as dry clay stores well, and can be mixed in the appropriate quantities when needed. Mixing dry clay can be a bit of a learning curve, so for beginners it's best to buy ready-to-use, moist clay in the bag.

Each clay has its own temperature range specification, so different clays need to be fired at different temperatures.

Clays are classified as low fire, mid-range, or high fire clays.

Earthenware clays are typically fired at lower temperatures, while stoneware and porcelain are fired at mid-to high fire temperatures. It's important to remember which clay you are using, and to note the correct firing temperature, since under or overfiring will cause cracking and potentially ruin your work.

HARVESTING YOUR OWN CLAY FROM SOIL

Humans have been making pottery for millennia, and before the advent of convenient hobby shops, clay was harvested directly from the soil. This enabled the making of earthenware pottery from materials collected from the local environment.

Clay is present in most environments, and even sandy soils can contain up to 20% clay. Your yield will naturally be higher if you look for high clay content soils. To find clay in your local environment, look for places where water doesn't drain well, or where soil becomes cracked when it's dry. Underneath the layer of topsoil, there will often be a dense layer of clay.

In the dry season or during droughts, you may be able to find clay in creek or river beds. You could also look in places where soil has been eroded or dug away, such as at construction sites. Be sure to get permission from the landowner or manager first.

To test the amount of clay present in your soil, fill a jar halfway with soil, then add water, and stir to break up the particles. The sand and silt will settle at the bottom after a few minutes, and the particles that remain suspended in the water make up the clay content.

There are two ways of processing naturally harvested clay; these are dry and wet processing. For dry processing, dry out the clay completely, and then crush the pieces with a mallet. Sieve out any organic matter such as stones, roots, or other impurities. The remaining clay powder can then be rehydrated as needed, though you might need to add some sand to add strength, and make it more resistant to cracking.

For wet processing, fill a container ⅓ with harvested clay, then fill to the top with water as for the clay test. Break up the clumps with your hands, and then leave the mixture to settle. Using a glass container allows you to see the separate layers.

Pour off the top layer of water, then carefully pour the clay layer into a fresh bucket, taking care not to let any sediment into the clay mix. Add more water, and allow to rest for several hours. The clay will settle into a dense layer at the bottom. Strain this through several layers of cloth until it is dry enough to work with.

CLAY STATES IN THE POTTERY-MAKING PROCESS

- **Wet Clay:** This is mixed clay that is ready to use. The clay is at its most elastic in this state.

- **Leather Hard:** At this stage of drying, a clay object can be handled without being deformed, but is still pliable enough to make changes to the form. This is the state in which trimming will most often be done.

- **Greenware:** pottery which is still in the drying process, and has not been fired yet.

- **Bone-dry:** the state at which the clay is ready to be fired. The clay is completely air dry, and extremely fragile. At this stage, the clay still contains about 15% of chemically bonded water.

- **Bisqueware:** pottery that has undergone its first firing. Pottery in this state will be porous, allowing for glaze solutions to adhere to the piece.

- **Ceramic:** clay that has been fired at high temperatures. During the firing process, the chemical composition of the clay changes permanently, and it will no longer dissolve in water.

- **Vitrified Clay:** Vitrification is the process whereby the silica in the clay is turned into glass by the firing process.

GROG IN CLAY

Grog is pre-fired pottery which has been ground up, with textures ranging from fine to coarse. It can be made from ceramic that has been fired for the purpose of making grog, or recycled from pottery broken by accident. It contains a high percentage of alumina and silica.

Grog is added to clay to add strength and reduce plasticity, which encourages superior drying, and reduces shrinkage. It also reduces the chances of cracking during both the drying and firing processes. All ceramics will shrink by about six percent while drying, and the size of the clay particles determines the amount of shrinkage. The ideal amount of grog is between seven and nine percent.

The larger grog particles reduce thermal expansion, which is the process of expanding and contracting while being fired in the kiln. Grog also improves permeability, as it allows water to channel the surface more easily without obstruction. Grog can add texture to finished ceramic pieces, and can also affect the way glazes turn out.

In handbuilding, a decent amount of added grog or sand provides strength to clay and reduces shrinkage. Since grog makes the clay more workable, it's great for sculptors, since it encourages the clay to hold its shape much better.

Grog also provides strength to wheel-thrown clay, but can be quite abrasive on your hands. The more grog a clay has, the rougher it will be to use, which can be difficult for beginner potters. A finer grog provides strength without hurting the potter's hands.

The best size for most purposes is 30/80—this means it will go through a mesh with 30 openings per inch, but not one with 80 openings per inch.

Porcelain clay should have a higher ratio of grog added, ranging between 5% and 30%. This encourages a quicker air-drying time, and reduces the chance of cracking during firing.

Grog encourages faster firing, so you may need to adjust the firing temperature of your clay accordingly. Commercial grog nearly always contains some iron, so it may not be suitable for adding to white clay.

STAGES OF DRYING

The stages of drying are wet, damp, soft leather hard, leather hard, stiff leather hard, dry, and bone-dry.

Leather hard clay is still visibly damp (it will be a darkish gray color) but is dry enough to handle without deforming the clay body. It can be gouged or incised without breaking, but won't take impressions in this state.

Soft leather hard is the best stage to attach a handle, as the clay is optimal for scoring, coating on slip, and joining two pieces together.

Medium leather hard is good for applying decorating techniques, carving, burnishing, and adding underglazes or slips.

During the hard leather hard stage is when you will be able to scrape off any excess clay to tidy up a piece.

At the bone-dry stage, your clay body becomes extremely fragile. The coloring will appear much lighter. Any work you do on the piece at this stage is known as fettling. This can produce a lot of dust, and it's recommended to wear a mask. Your clay body is ready for firing when it's bone-dry.

SHRINKAGE AND WEIGHT LOSS

Clay will shrink while it dries, as well as during firing. Different clay bodies have different rates of shrinkage; this can vary from 4% to 15%. In selecting a clay type and design of the piece you have in mind, you need to take into account the rate of shrinkage at the appropriate firing temperature.

If you are working to a specific end-size specification, you might want to make a shrinkage ruler; this will help you determine the size the piece should be when wet.

Most clays are composed of around 20% water and 9% organic matter, and will therefore lose around 30% of their weight after being fired.

CAUSES OF S-CRACKS

The process of drying clay is very important, and has to be done correctly, otherwise pieces may crack while being fired. Clay bodies need to be dried out slowly and carefully. If they dry too quickly, this causes stress in the clay, making it fragile and prone to cracks. Even the smallest crack may get bigger during firing. If your piece is not dry enough, it can crack while in the kiln.

Clay shrinks as it dries, and if one part dries faster than another, this puts the clay under stress. It's not uncommon for the walls of a vessel to dry out faster than the base, since the sides are more exposed to air. This is especially true when pottery is left to dry on its base on a solid surface, since there is no airflow over the underside.

So-called "S-cracks" can occur as a result of stress, when the walls of the vessel dry out faster than the base. These 'S' shaped cracks appear at the base of a piece, and can vary in depth and size. They may not go all the way through, and may only be visible from one side.

If the clay at the base of the vessel is thicker than the sides, this contributes further to slower drying, and the danger of cracks forming. The bottom edge of a vessel where the sides meet the base often tends to be thicker.

The base is also prone to having a higher moisture content, because water collects on the inside during the throwing process. Even if you mop up the water on the inside with a sponge (and it's imperative that you do so) the clay at the bottom will be wetter. This means that the base has fewer clay particles as compared to the walls, resulting in a lower density and strength.

During the throwing process, the walls and rim of the vessel are in almost continuous contact with your hands, which aligns the clay particles. As the clay dries, the particles shrink across their width at a greater rate than across their length. Since the particles in the walls are well-aligned, they all shrink in the same direction.

The particles in the base, by contrast, have had much less contact with your hands and are therefore only partially aligned. Their more random positioning means that they shrink in different directions. The base of the piece therefore shrinks less in volume than the walls.

While S-cracks can occur in any type of wheel-thrown piece, plates are more susceptible to cracking due to the larger distance between the rim and the center of the base. This creates more stress on the base.

HOW TO AVOID S-CRACKS

If you are having trouble with cracks appearing in your thrown pieces, there are a couple of techniques you can try to remedy this.

- **Wedging**. Always make sure that your clay is well-wedged. Spiral wedging produces a cone-like seashell shape, and it's common to put the wider end on the wheel with the cone pointing upwards. Some potters hold that the join between the spiral layers can create a point of weakness, which can make the formation of S-cracks more likely. For this reason, spiral-wedged clay should be turned on its side; the base of the cone shouldn't form the base of the vessel.

- **Throwing the clay on the wheel.** You could also try throwing or dropping clay onto the wheel with some force before centering. The reasoning behind this technique is that the force of throwing the clay onto the wheel starts the process of aligning the clay particles.

- **Use a porous bat**. A plaster bat is porous, and helps to draw some moisture out of the base, whereas the metal wheelhead is non-absorbent. Using a bat also allows you to leave the pot on the bat to dry after you've thrown it. The bat will continue to draw moisture from the base as the vessel dries.

- **Avoid making the base very thick**. Check the thickness of the base with a needle tool, and aim for the base to be the same thickness as the walls. Remember that you will lose some thickness when slicing off the wheel head or bat, and during the trimming process.

- **Trim off extra clay off the base**. If the base is quite thick, you might want to trim it twice; once while the piece is still damp, and a second time when its leather hard.

- **Compressing the base**. Spend some time compressing the base after opening the form, moving your fingers inwards, and stopping when you get to the middle. This compresses the clay particles together. If you move from the center outwards, you will be stretching the clay particles apart.

- **Cut your piece off the bat.** Always cut off the bat before setting aside to dry, as this reduces pressure on the base.

- **Turn the pot over to dry**. When it's firm enough to do so without deforming the shape, turn your point over to dry. Exposing the base to more airflow helps to even out the drying process. This also helps to prevent the foot from becoming deformed.

- **Drying on a wire rack.** Using a wire rack promotes even air flow and drying, especially for large flat pieces such as plates.

- **Keep your pots covered with plastic.** This encourages slow and even drying. Gradually loosen the plastic as the pieces dry, and eventually remove them completely.

- **Beating the base.** Depending on the form, tap it with your hand or a piece of curved wood. This helps to compress and align the clay particles. You can make your own homemade tool for the job.

4

WEDGING CLAY AND
REPURPOSING CLAY SCRAPS

Wedging clay is arguably the most important part of pottery-making, and is something you will be doing a lot of! Wedging is a fundamental pottery skill, and learning at least one method is essential. This process ensures that any hard lumps or air bubbles are eliminated from the clay, creating a uniform consistency which makes it more manageable, and reliable to work with. Wedging clay must be done before starting any pottery form on the wheel.

Learning to wedge clay can be a tricky skill to master for beginners. While the goal is to remove air bubbles and create a homogeneous mass, beginners may end up wedging more air in than they take out! Rest assured that you will get better with practice. There are a few different methods of wedging, and these include the ram's head method, spiral wedging, and wire wedging.

The height of your wedging table should be low enough for you to be able to lean in with your body weight. If your table is a bit too high, keep a few wooden boards on hand to stand on, and lift yourself up a bit. Wedging is much easier to do if you maximize your upper body weight to help push down, rather than just your arms.

If you are using concrete board, it's advisable to mist the surface to counter the absorption, as the clay will stick otherwise.

The ram head method is usually the easiest for beginners to learn. Start with a chunk that feels comfortable in your hands; a smaller amount is better to start with if you're new at wedging. Work the clay in your hands for a short while, then throw it down onto the board, flattening it into a square.

*1. Holding the front of the block of clay with both hands, begin
to knead the clay by pushing down and forward with the palms
of your hands,*

*2. and then pulling the clay back onto itself from the top.
Repeat steps 1 and 2, pushing the clay down and forward, and
then pulling the clay back. The motion is very similar to
needing dough.*

*Do this several times, pushing the clay down and forward, and
then pulling it back, until the top of the clay resembles a
rounded 'ram's head' shape.*

P at in the sides, and roll the whole piece up into a solid roll, compressing with your hands as you do so.

Use a wire tool to cut the clay in half to check for air bubbles. If there are none, you can pound the two pieces back together, and wedge a few more times before use. If you won't be using it for several days, store the wedge clay in heavy duty plastic bags, or freezer bags for small quantities. Store the bags inside a container with a tight-fitting lid, such as a plastic tub.

Spiral wedging can be tricky to master, but this method allows you to wedge small amounts of clay very quickly. It's similar to the ram's head method, except that you press and fold the clay in a spiral motion, with spirals decreasing in size. Pushing down and lifting the clay up with a slight rotation incorporates a small amount of new clay with each fold.

You may sometimes want to use some of your softer, reclaimed clay to mix into other, firmer clay to soften it. When mixing clay of varying firmness, it's a good idea to get them into the same shaped block first, as this makes it easier to layer them. Slice layers of each block alternately, using your wire tool, and layer them on top of each other.

Cut wedging is a useful method for wedging larger lumps of clay, and is less exerting than spiral wedging. Use a wire tool to slice through the layered block, then slam one half of the layers down onto the other. Slice through again and repeat; for every repetition, you will double the amount of layers. Flip the block, and hit it onto the table,; then turn it over and repeat.

RECLAIMING CLAY SCRAPS

Whether you are hand-building or wheel-throwing, it's inevitable that you will accumulate clay scraps. As a beginner potter, you will go through a lot of practice clay. The good news is that this can be recycled into usable clay. You should have a reclaim bucket at hand for all your clay scraps to go into, or more than one if you are working with different types of clay.

If you make a mistake while throwing a piece, it's often best to put it in your reclaim bucket before trying to use it again, as it will be too soft to throw again immediately.

Reclaiming clay is made easier by working with smaller batches at a time, and having the bucket on wheels helps you move it around more easily. A bucket that will hold around 40 pounds of clay is ideal.

You may want to sort scraps by color or working properties, such as hand-building versus throwing. When working with white clay, check that buckets, tools, working surfaces and towels are free of other clay bodies or ceramic colorants, to keep them white.

Scraps from throwing are likely to be quite wet, and will include slurry. These can be added to your reclaim bucket as you work. Thinner trimmings can go straight into your slurry bucket, but larger pieces will need to be dried out completely and broken up. If your scraps from hand-building are not dried out too much, you can compress them back together, and wedge them again before use.

Wheel-throwing will generate more fine particles than large particles, and these fine particles contained in your throwing water need to be reclaimed as well, to maintain the proper composition of your clay.

When your scrap bucket is halfway full, switch to a new bucket. Break down larger, dried-out pieces into smaller chunks, as these will slake down faster. Fill the bucket with water, covering the clay with a few inches. You may need to add more water to cover the clay as the water gets absorbed. Monitor the condition of the reclaim by checking on it frequently, and aim to keep the liquid level above the solid level.

The scraps will quickly slake into a slurry; let this settle for several hours, or even a few days. If a layer of water forms on top, you can pour this off (disposing of this water outside will be better for your plumbing in the long term). Mix through thoroughly until no big lumps remain. Transfer this into a wide plastic container, such as a plastic storage tub.

Put the container somewhere out of the way for a few days where it won't get bumped or spilled, checking on it every day, and giving it a stir. The slurry will slowly dry to a thicker, sludge-like consistency; it will be thick but not quite solid.

Turn this out onto a plasterboard or bat to dry out further. Avoid putting plaster bats onto any wooden surface, as these can turn moldy quite quickly. You can even build a stack of alternating plaster bats and clay; a stack of six 9 x 12 inch plaster slabs will process 40 pounds of clay.

Once you've piled the clay on the bat, smooth it out with your hand to allow for even drying, so you don't end up with some bits that are drier than others. These can become difficult to mix in later on.

After a day or two, flip the slab of clay over, so that the other side can begin to dry out. The length of this process can vary according to the seasons; on a hot summer's day, you might be able to flip the clay on the same day, while in winter it might take a few days.

If you don't have a bat, and will only do this occasionally, (or to speed up the drying process) you can use some old towels designated for the purpose. Spread the clay out on towels outside to a thickness of 2 to 3 inches, and let it dry. In hot weather this may only take an hour or two.

When you can form the clay into a ball without it sticking to your hands, start scraping it off the towels gently. You can use a plastic putty knife for this. If using plasterboard, make sure there are no plaster particles stuck in the clay.

At this stage the clay will still be soft, and you can work it with your hands, or on a piece of canvas to dry it out further. If you plan to use the clay for throwing, then it needs to be wedged first, to remove any trapped air, and to promote a homogeneous consistency.

HOW MANY TIMES CAN YOU RECLAIM CLAY?

There is no limit to the number of times your clay can be reclaimed, if you do so with care. Over time, the clay may become gritty and loose its plasticity. You can revive your clay by adding a teaspoon of Epsom salts per gallon of water, being sure to dissolve the salts before adding it to your clay.

5

CENTERING, CONING, AND RAISING THE WALLS

CENTERING CLAY ON THE WHEEL

Centering your clay can be tricky to master, but as with anything, the key to improvement is practice. The success of the throwing process rests on getting the clay as centered as possible. Don't be disheartened if you don't get it right the first time!

It's best to wear short sleeves when throwing on the wheel, to keep your hands and arms free to move. Make sure your body is in the right position: position your legs as close to the splash pan or wheel as possible, keeping your arms anchored, and your back straight. Stop and rest from time to time, as repetitive motion over long periods can lead to muscle and joint strain.

Having a good potter's stool can also make a big difference. You can also set up your wheel to the right height to throw while standing if it's uncomfortable, or you find that it hurts your back to do so sitting down.

For beginners, clay with some grog or sand in it is preferable, as it takes longer to center and bring up the walls. If your clay is too smooth and worked on for too long, it's likely to collapse. If the clay is too stiff, it will require more strength and pressure to form. Be sure to keep your clay well sealed to keep it moist, by storing in plastic bags or wrap. If your clay is too hard, spray some water on it, and wedge it well.

When your clay has been properly wedged, round the clay into a ball in your hands to ensure that it will spread evenly across the center of the wheel. Turn the ball over in your hands, and check for any cracks in the clay where air could get trapped. You want to avoid this happening, as air pockets will throw your clay out of alignment, and you will not be able to get it centered.

If you notice any cracks, spend some time kneading the clay, smoothing out any unevenness, and removing any air bubbles. Before putting clay on the wheel, make sure that it has a rounded bottom, not flat, as a flat surface increases the chances of air getting trapped.

Moisten the bat with your finger, and either throw or pat the clay into the center of the wheel. Before spinning the wheel, try to position the clay as close to the center as possible.

Press it down lightly with the palm of your hand to fix it in place. Wet your hands, and douse the clay with a bit of water or slurry. If the clay gets dry, it will catch on your hands and go off center.

The wheel should be spinning at medium-high to full speed. Keep a sponge in your right hand so you can squeeze a bit of water on the clay if needed. Press into the sides of the clay with your hands, smoothing at the base of the ball with the fingers of your right hand, using the left hand to steady the right hand. This seals the clay to the wheel head.

TECHNIQUES FOR CENTERING

Potters will often use different methods for centering clay on the wheel. This is a matter of preference, and finding which method works best for you.

In the western hemisphere, the default direction of the wheel is counter-clockwise (in the East it is primarily clockwise). This means that the main thrust of the clay will be going towards the left, and so this is where you will do most of the initial work. If you hold your hand against the clay on the left, the clay will center itself quite quickly.

The traditional method for centering, taught in many pottery classes, is to center the clay with the heel (or wrist) of one hand and either the flat or the fist of the other hand.

Brace the elbow of your left hand against your body (or the side of the splash pan). Using the palm of your left wrist, press into the wobbling clay. Lean into the clay, utilizing your left wrist to stabilize the form. If your arm is being pushed back and forth, the clay will not become centered. Brace your elbow so that you will not be pushed by the clay.

position the blade of your right hand over the surface of the clay, as if you were going to give it a karate chop. You can use a karate chop hand position or a fist. As you lean into the clay with your left wrist, push downwards against the clay with your right hand to help stabilize the form.

Note: If you are struggling to gain control over the spinning clay, check your elbows! If they are far away from your body they will not be able to stabilize the clay. You should use your body as an anchor for your arms as they are being pushed against by the clay. The more centered your body is, the more centered the clay will become.

After pushing the clay downwards, you will likely still have a wobbling piece. Continue to lean into the clay with your left wrist, and then take your right hand to the outside of the form, resting the edge of your hand on top of the wheel-head. Begin pulling the clay into the braced, left wrist. You should aim to push into the clay with your left hand, while pulling the clay towards the left wrist with your right hand. It is a push and pull motion that will guide the clay into the middle of the wheel. Pushing forward with the left, and pulling the clay into the left hand with the right. It is an opposite act that will stabilize the form.

CONING THE FORM

As you center, depending on the size of the clay, you may struggle to get the form fully centered. Many potters will also include a step called coning, or wheel-wedging. This is done to incorporate a bit more water if the clay is very stiff, or just to homogenize the clay. Coning eliminates any lingering inconsistencies and air bubbles that might have been missed during wedging. Coning is a technique that can be added to the centering process. Coning also acts as another form of wedging and can further help to get air bubbles out of the form. It's recommended to do three cycles of this to properly align the clay particles.

If you wish to cone your form you will lean into the clay with your left wrist, and pull the clay with your right hand into your left wrist.

Use your upper body weight to lean in with your left hand, applying pressure on the side of the clay so that it rises up as it rotates. As you push the clay, and pull it towards you, the clay will start to raise upwards. Allow the clay to rise into a cone, towards the center of the wheel.

*When the clay cones into the middle, take your right hand into
a fist, pushing straight down into the center of the cone,
pushing the clay towards the wheel head. The clay will be
forced inward by the heel of your left hand, while the other
hand forces the top of the dome down.*

*As you guide the clay back towards the wheel-head , you will
want to relax the pressure from your left hand. This alternating
pressure creates the up-and-down movement that eases the clay
into the center. The top of the form will begin to "mushroom
over", so as the form gets closer to the wheel-head, begin
pressing into the form with the wrist of your left hand to hinder
the "mushrooming" of the top, as well as continuing to add
stability to your form.*

SLAP CENTERING

Some potters will use a technique called "slap centering,"
using both hands to slap the clay into the center, and then
seal down the clay to the wheel head.

To do this, center the clay into a dome shape, and push into the middle, forcing it upward into a tall cone shape. With your arm braced securely, use your right hand to brace the clay, while the left hand pushes down on the top of the cone, flattening it. As you bring the clay back down, ensure that it swells from the inside out rather than folding over onto itself, and then reform the dome.

You can use a modeling tool to check if your clay is centered. Place the pointed end against the clay, holding it steady with both hands while you turn the wheel. If there is a line only on one side, then you will be able to see where you are off center. Cone the clay back up a little, anchor your hand, and press down. If you see a thin line all the way around, your clay is centered, and you can proceed to the next step.

HOW WILL YOU KNOW IF THE CLAY IS CENTERED?

You'll know the clay is centered when you no longer feel any wobbles or movement under your hand as the clay rotates at full speed. It will also look as if it's standing still on the wheel.

While you are centering you should be thinking one step ahead as to what kind of form you are intending to make. You will want to think of the base an how wide it will need to be. If you are making a low, wide, form such as a plate or shallow bowl, you should center the clay into a low, wide dome.

If you are making a pot with fairly equal dimensions, center the clay into an average dome shape, with the dome mirroring a similar dimension of the base of your piece. Bear in mind that your fingers should be able to reach all the way down to the form's floor as you open it, so starting with a tall dome is not recommended.

COMMON CENTERING PROBLEMS

You will need to practice many times before centering becomes second nature to you. You may want to take a pottery class to help you master this skill. This will help you eliminate any bad habits, and speed up your learning process. Some common problems you might encounter are as follows:

- **You're using the wrong clay.** Choose a smooth clay that has good plasticity. As a beginner, a softer clay will be easier to center, but it shouldn't be so soft that it loses its shape when you pull up the walls.

- **Your clay hasn't been wedged properly**. If you encounter hard spots, or if there is an air pocket in the clay, then it hasn't been wedged properly. This can throw the clay off center. To avoid air pockets, make sure the clay is rounded at the bottom, and not flat when you put it on the wheel. Be sure to wedge your clay properly to ensure a uniform consistency.

- **Your elbows are in the air**. This gives you far less control over the clay. Keep them anchored to your body.

- **You're pushing too hard.** This will cause your clay to go off center. Using your whole body, and letting your hands steer makes this easier on your hands, arms, and back.

- **You get a mushroom or volcano effect.** This can create a pocket where air or slip can get trapped. If this happens, cone up the clay, then push down with the heel of your hand, keeping your anchor hand firm.

- **Your wheel is moving too slowly**. It needs to spin at a medium-high or high speed for centering.

- **Your clay goes off center when you remove your hand.** This happens to most new potters. It's important to remove your hand slowly and gently, as the mound can easily be knocked off center by any jerky hand movements.

- **You aren't keeping your elbows in, against your side.** The farther your elbows are from your waist, the less stability you will have to center the clay

- **You are letting the clay bully you.** Don't let the clay guide you and push you around. Instead of focusing on trying to catch the clay spinning around the wheel, focus on your body positioning. Keep your arms firm, elbows in, and lean into the clay with a firm palm. This will show the clay where to go, rather than the clay showing you.

OPENING THE CLAY

Now that your clay has been properly centered, you can proceed to opening up the vessel. This is also commonly referred to as "dropping the middle." There are two parts to this process: making an opening in the center of the clay, and then opening out the space on the inside of the clay. Different potters will develop their own preference as to which fingers they prefer to use and how to position their hands. The principles remain the same, and once you have done this a few times, you will find what works best for you.

Start spinning the wheel at a medium speed. With your hands on either side of the clay, press slightly to make an indentation in the middle. Then press into the center with both hands together, Using one thumb to open the form, and the other hand to brace the thumb.

Press downward steadily, and make a hole in the center that's about half to a quarter inch from the bottom.

You want to leave enough space at the bottom of your clay body so that it has a nice foot.

When you are happy with the amount of space at the bottom, you need to widen the bottom of the vessel. Using both thumbs next to each other, begin pulling your hands apart, widening the hole.

As you widen the form, you will want to keep your thumbs flat and resist the urge of lifting your hands as you pull the center apart. The aim is creating a flat base, not a "U" shape. Aim for a flat floor with a 90° transition from the floor to the wall. This also creates a curve on the inside for you to grab onto as you go on to raising the walls in the next step.

As you widen, move your hands slowly apart. Opening the base should happen in one fluid motion. If you get a little hill in the center at the bottom, use your fingers or your sponge to press it down, moving back and forth over the middle and to the outside. This compresses the bottom, which will prevent it from cracking later.

The inner diameter that you are aiming for is contingent
upon what form you are making. You will want to pull
the base apart to the appropriate circumference of the
base of the form you are trying to make.

Note: If you are unsure of how thin the base is while opening the piece, your needle tool can help with this. Stop the wheel periodically to check the height of the foot by poking your needle tool into the floor. Stick the tool into the center of the hole, allowing your index finger to slide down the needle until it touches the clay, and then pull it out. The distance between the end of your finger, and the end of the needle will show you the thickness at the bottom. You want to aim for 1/3 inch of thickness.

RAISING THE WALLS

Raising the walls of your vessel can be one of the most difficult steps for beginners to learn. There are many different ways to raise or 'pull' the walls up, but getting your hands in the right position is crucial. One way is to use only the fingertips, leading with the longest finger. Pulling is essentially squeezing the inner walls of the clay body to force it to move up.

Start by having your left hand on the inside of the form, and right hand on the outside. You will want to rest your left arm against the side of your body, and rest your right forearm on your leg, leaning slightly to the right as you begin pulling. It is important to have the clay be wet the whole time you are working on your form.

Begin by using the tips of your middle and pointer finger on each hand. With the wheel spinning at a medium speed, you will want to start each pull as far down as possible on the piece. The point of pulling is to get the clay from the bottom of the cylinder all the way to the top. Pressing into the base of the wall, utilizing both inner and outer pressure, you should see a rim form above your right hand fingers.

Keeping that consistent pressure and speed of the wheel, pull the rim up to the top of the form. Move your hands slowly as you make your way to the top, so that you do not loose the rim you are pulling upwards.

Each pull should finish at the top of the piece and your fingers should touch at the top. That is a completed pull. If you stop the pulls too early, your form will likely become top heavy and inconsistent. Don't forget to add water between each pull.

Repeat the steps. Pressing into the base of the wall with your inner and outer hands, forming a rim above your finger tips, and pulling the rim up to the top of the form, until your fingers meet. Continue this until you have the height and thickness you are aiming for.

The goal is consistency. If you are altering the speed and pressure of your hands, you will have a lot of variations in the walls of your piece. If the form isn't raising, use more pressure in your finger tips. If the form is starting to become wavy and collapse on itself, lighten up your pressure.

As the form gets taller, it will become thinner, so you will need to loosen your pressure as you go. It will become very delicate the thinner it becomes.

To goal is to form a straight wall. Before you alter the shape or width of the form, create the height first. Height is always first before width, even when you are creating a bowl. Focusing first on building the walls will be the easiest way of having consistency in your forms, as pulling consistent walls on a sloped and shapely form will be challenging.

when you have the height you are happy with, you can move on to adding shape and personality to the form.

FURTHER INSIGHTS

K eeping your thumbs connected while pulling up the walls will help create stability, and allows your hands to move in unison. Bracing your right arm against your leg helps to keep your arm stable while you pull, so that you are only moving your arm from the elbow. If you find that you're lifting your elbow up as you are pulling, you will notice that it becomes much more difficult to pull the clay effectively, since there will be a lot more muscles involved that you have to control and steady!

For larger pieces you may want to use your knuckle instead of your finger tips, but for smaller pieces you can just use your fingertips. Compress the rim with your thumb when you get to the top to create a flat, even surface after each pull, resetting the rim after each movement helps to make sure that it stays centered.

Keeping the clay moist is essential, so that your fingers hydroplane over the surface of the clay without sticking. If it feels dry, you can stop the wheel and squeeze on a bit more water with your sponge, or wet your hands.

If you knock the clay off center by accident, or end up with uneven walls, use a straight-edged wooden rib on the outside, holding your left finger at a 90-degree angle pointing downward on the inside. Spin the wheel slowly, guiding the clay slowly and steadily back to a uniform thickness.

If the rim develops a wobble, you can either cut it off using your needle tool, or you can use a technique called the "claw grip" to eliminate any undulations. Support the clay with your right hand, allowing the rim to run between your two right forefingers, pressing down and squeezing gently. This will effectively recenter the rim without having to cut off a piece.

COMMON PULLING PROBLEMS

As a beginner potter, you may be unsure of how many pulls you need to perform to raise the walls of your vessel sufficiently. The ideal is to do this in as few pulls as possible, since pulling too many times can overstress the clay, and weaken the integrity of your vessel. But rather than focusing on how many pulls it's done in, your goal should be getting the walls to the proper thickness and height.

Some common problems you may encounter when you first start pulling up your cylinder include:

- **Making the walls too thin.** This happens when you put too much pressure on the top versus the bottom. The greatest amount of pressure is needed at the bottom of the piece to pull the clay up evenly, and you should gradually release the pressure as you reach the top.

- **Wrinkling at the top**. This is most often because there is a thin spot, and a wrinkle appears because it has lost strength in that area. The remedy for this is to compress the area using a flexible metal rib tool.

- **The clay body begins to twist and warp.** If you keep too much pressure on one spot, this can

create a weak section. This is a sign that you need
to move your hands upwards a bit faster.

- **Stopping midway through a pull.** Beginner
  potters will often stop and start again at the point
  where they stopped. This will cause the walls to
  thin out unevenly, and collapse. Each pull needs to
  be completed from top to bottom, even if you
  don't feel it's very good.

TEN TIPS FOR IMPROVED THROWING

1. Start the wheel spinning before putting your
   hands on the clay.
2. Avoid making any jerky movements with your
   hands, or sudden changes in wheel speed, as this
   can throw the pot off center.
3. Start with smaller amounts of clay. If you're not
   able to execute a form successfully with two
   pounds of clay, you won't have more success with
   a greater amount.
4. Keep your throwing lines close together; they
   should be around one eighth of an inch apart.
   When pulling up, do so relative to the wheel speed;
   the slower the speed, the slower you should

ascend. Reduce the wheel speed as you go up, and when working on wide forms.

5. Make sure that your clay is well-lubricated at all times. If the clay gets dry, your hands will stick to the clay, causing friction and drag. This leads to twists and wrinkles in the clay. Too much water, though, and your pot will get soggy and weak.

6. Aim for uniformity in the thickness of the walls, and avoid thin spots. This is achieved by keeping steady pressure with your fingers, and keeping the gap between your fingers even.

7. If you intend to trim a pot, make sure that the rim is level. Cut off the rim with your needle tool if needed.

8. No matter which direction the wheel is spinning, your fingers should always be pointing away from the direction the clay is moving, rather than towards it; otherwise your fingers will dig into the clay.

9. Practice making tall cylinders. The more you practice pulling up the walls, the better you will get at it.

10. Observe your pots, and note where you have succeeded and where not. Consider the width of the foot relative to the neck and rim, and whether the form looks balanced.

6

THROWING BOWLS

Throwing a bowl is one of the first things you should learn to make, right after you've learned centering. This introduces you to the methods for forming your shape after making your cylinder. Making a cylinder, and forming it outwards, is one of the basic things you need to know to create almost any other shape on the wheel. Bowls are the simplest project to make, and most of your accidents will probably turn into bowls!

Prepare your clay by wedging it thoroughly, and then weigh out the pieces needed. If you are making more than one bowl, portion the clay into lumps of around a pound each, and wedge each of the lumps as well to make sure they have a rounded bottom.

Making use of plaster-throwing bats attached to leather

hard pads of clay on the wheel will make it easier to lift the completed bowl off the wheel.

Begin by centering and open the clay, leaving a thickness at the base of 1.5 cm. Centering, coning and raising the walls all are similar steps with throwing a bowl, the main difference comes at the end of building the height on your piece. You will start by making a cylinder, making sure to even the walls and the rim.

It's best to keep the cylinder thicker at the base than it really needs to be, and also slightly wider, as the excess can be trimmed away later. Leave too much rather than too little, to ensure you have enough material to work with when creating the foot. The foot section should be wide enough so that when trimmed, the base will be stable, and won't rock from side to side. The width of the foot will depend on the shape and size of the bowl you are making, the clay type you are using, and the intended function of the bowl.

Once you have the height that you are aiming for, as you are completing your last wall pull you will start to bring the piece outwards, away from the middle. This will happen within the final pull. Your inner hand will start to become more dominant and will guide the clay outwards, with curved fingers and starting from the base, slowly raise the wall outwards away from the middle.

F ocus on the internal shape rather than the external, since the outside can be trimmed later. You want to try and avoid having to trim on the inside, as this can be tedious, because trimmings will fall onto your trimming tool as you're working. You can use a soft rubber rib on the inside of the cylinder to stretch it outwards. You can even use an old CD to gently scrape the inside to make it smooth. Remember that when you aren't able to brace against the splash pan, you need to brace with your other hand.

Don't worry about the throwing lines, or any slip or water that accumulates in the bowl, as this can be sponged out before taking the bowl off the wheel.

When you are happy with the shape, begin refining the form with a curved metal rib. Push the curved edge gently into the base, and run it up the walls of the bowl, following with your fingers on the inside. The metal rib will scrape off all the loose clay, and encourage the perfect self-supporting curvature.

A metal rib is ideal for this because of its hardness and flexibility, while a wooden rib is hard but not flexible. The metal rib removes the majority of slip and sticky clay which aids in the drying process.

Some throwing rings in the upper walls can add to the final aesthetic, but you want the base of the pot to be as smooth and rounded as possible. This is also where glaze will most accumulate.

Compact the rim with your sponge, running it through your fingers, or your fingers, gently pinching with the left hand and pressing downwards with the right. This strengthens the lip of the bowl. You can also use a chamois cloth to soften the rim, and give it a soft beveled edge.

You will want to remove some of the excess clay from the bottom to neaten up the form, since very wet clay can take a lot longer to dry out.

If the top of the bowl is uneven, use a needle tool placed at an angle on the outside of the bowl just below the uneven area. You will want to hold your hand steady as the wheel spins while you insert the needle. The tendency is to want to follow the piece as it spins, but resist this urge and hold your hand steady, allowing the spinning wheel to slice the top off rather than you cutting the piece. When the needle tool goes all the way through you can lift off the top layer of the rim. Use a sponge to smooth out the upper edge.

Scrape any excess slip off the wooden bat. To remove the finished bowl from the wheel, use a twisted metal wire, pulling this very taut before sliding underneath the pot. The wire needs to stay flat the entire time, to prevent it from cutting away any clay from the bowl intended for the foot ring. Pry the bat off the wheel, and set aside to dry.

When using a throwing bat, many potters will usually leave the piece on the bat to dry somewhat before removing it. However, there may be times when you want to take the pot off the bat immediately. Squeeze some water onto the bat in front of the pot with your sponge. Then run your wire tool under the pot, together with some of the water, until the pot starts to move. Remove the bat from the wheel, tilt it slightly and gently slide the pot off the bat. (Note that you shouldn't use this method if using a plaster bat).

If you are throwing for practice, slice your bowl in half vertically to check for uniformity and thickness of the walls and base. This can tell you a lot about how hard you're pulling, and gives you an inside look at how you can improve your technique.

7

THROWING MUGS

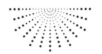

I n this chapter, we cover the process for throwing mugs. A mug is one of the easiest forms to learn to throw on the wheel, since it is basically just a small cylinder with a rounded belly and a handle attached. However, there are some basic design elements to consider, and this can make throwing a mug a bit more challenging than it first appears.

When throwing a mug, consider the four parts that make up the form; the foot, the body, the rim, and the handle. Consider each part separately first, and then note whether they work together to make up a cohesive unit. It's important to factor in good proportions of each element, to achieve cohesiveness and balance.

Start with a smallish amount of wedged clay; around one and a quarter pounds should be enough. Pat the clay into a rounded shape, or roll on a smooth clean surface into a point. Wet the surface of the wheel, then slap the clay point side down, as close to the center as possible.

Open the clay, and compress the floor using the two middle fingers of your right hand, or a small potter's rib, sliding left and right and up and down, and taking care not to apply too much pressure. This will prevent any S-cracks in the future.

*Aim for uniformity of the walls from bottom to top, and avoid
making the rim too wide until you have done the former;
otherwise it will be difficult to remedy later. While a chunkier
mug can serve as a good hand warmer, it can feel too heavy to
hold.*

*Pull up the walls of your cylinder; since this is a small piece,
you can just use your fingers.*

When you have the desired height, use a hard plastic rib to compress the walls. Using a hard rib will get rid of any throwing lines, and straighten the cylinder walls. You can also use a metal rib to get rid of throwing lines and compress the walls.

Angle the rib at the bottom of the cylinder, and follow the rib up and down with your fingers on the inside wall, smoothing out the throw lines on the outside, and beginning to shape the curve of the mug.

I f using your flexible metal rib tool to shape the mug you can massage the walls from the inside into the curve of the rib, creating a smooth bellied curve. Then, continue shaping the wall above the curve.

To save some time with dry trimming later, do your trimming while the mug is still on the wheel. Using a plastic or wooden knife tool, with the point and blade edge pointed down, begin to peel off layers of clay that are too thick and unnecessary. Then, use a needle or wooden knife tool to remove the small ring of clay created around the bottom of the cylinder, adding your clay scraps to your reclaim bucket as you go.

When you are satisfied with your form you will want to

reach into the vessel with your sponge to soak up the water that has gathered at the bottom. You can also soften the inside throw lines with a sponge.

Compress the rim with your sponge, or fingers, pinching gently with one hand and pressing down lightly on the rim to smooth it out, this also makes the rim a bit thicker.

Finally, cut the mug from the wheel or bat using your wire tool, and set aside to dry.

COMMON BEGINNER PROBLEMS WHEN THROWING A MUG

While there are unlimited possibilities when choosing a design for your mug, considering the individual elements and how they work together will improve both the aesthetic as well as the functionality of the piece. Some common problems you may encounter when starting out with throwing a mug are the following:

- **The mug is too squat**. Since a potter's view of the form being created is primarily from above, it's important to lean down to check the shape of the profile. A squat-shaped mug may have a rim that flares out, thick walls, and a thick bottom. This adds unwanted weight, and the uneven distribution of the clay can lead to cracking when drying.

If the width of the foot is much smaller than the width of the rim, this throws off the balance of the mug. The width and diameter of the rim is also essential to how the mug will flow. In this instance, try pushing the floor gently outwards, where the floor meets the wall. This will help to even out the severe lines. Be wary of undercutting the wall when doing this, as this can make the mug more difficult to clean. If the foot becomes too narrow, it can be difficult to fix, and it's best to start over.

- **Vase-shaped mug.** In this instance, the rim will have been pulled out too far, and be too thin. If the rim is wider than the rest of the body, this increases the chances of warping during firing. A thin rim, coupled with the steep angle of the neck, doubles the chances of that area breaking easily, and it also affects the liquid flow of the mug. There may also be a severe angle from where the bottom bellies out, and where the neck begins to curve outward, which makes the mug look out of proportion.

Compress the rim to strengthen it and thicken the walls, gently pulling the wall inward to lessen the severe angle. Use a rib to push out the neck, and improve flow to the bellied-out section. Continue making small adjustments to the contours while making sure that the rim is thickening. If the bottom is still too thick, extend the height by pulling up the clay again.

- **The globe mug**. Beginner potters may tend to overextend the clay shape when trying to make a mug that holds a lot of volume. From the top, the rim will appear much narrower than the body. If the rim is cinched in too much, it will affect the functionality and flow of the liquid, leading to a mug that dribbles. To fix this, first push the body inward so that it's in better proportion to the rest of the piece. Form a neck at the top by shortening the body, and leaving a section at the top of the mug. Then, shape the neck so that it's in proportion. If the foot is still too wide, trim away some clay from the foot, and add a notched profile.

- **Making a tumbler.** When making this form, beginners may have trouble keeping the rim from flaring outward. If the rim is wider than the body, this poses a risk of breakage. The wide rim will also allow liquid to flow out faster, and potentially cause it to dribble. The foot will also be too narrow to support the tall piece, making it unbalanced and unstable. In this case, it's better just to start over. You can still add some flare to the body without letting the rim get too wide. Ensuring the foot is wider in proportion to the rest of the tumbler gives it more stability.

8
PULLING AND ATTACHING HANDLES

Now that you've learned how to throw a mug, you'll need to know how to shape and attach handles. There are several different methods for making handles, and we'll look at a few of these in depth. In all instances, your clay vessel should be leather hard before attaching your handle—firm but with a bit of springiness. If it bends out of shape easily with a slight squeeze, then it's still too soft. If it has no moisture left and is too dry to trim, then it is too hard.

Your handle should be the same thickness and clay body as the walls of the vessel it will be attached to, or you may encounter problems due to differences in the shrinkage rate. The handle should also be dry enough to form a gentle curve when held before attaching.

METHODS FOR MAKING HANDLES

The easiest and quickest types of handles to make are the strap and coil varieties. These are either cut from a slab, or rolled out into a coil. A coil is a piece of clay that has been rolled, and then flattened into a shape resembling a carrot; it should be slightly thicker at one end than the other. The thicker end will usually be attached at the top of the vessel. You essentially will form the handle just by cutting out clay. There are also handle pulling tools that you can buy to create a handle. These are all options, but let's explore the traditional method of pulling handles.

PULLING HANDLES

While strap and coil handles are the easiest to make, it's worth learning how to make a pulled handle, as these have a more organic feel, and more fluid lines. The action of pulling the clay also aligns the clay particles, making the handle stronger.

A handle can be pulled in two ways, directly on a cylinder, or by itself, before being cut to fit and then attached.

To begin, wedge the clay to make sure it's free of air bubbles. Then form a carrot shape with your hands, making it a bit more oval than round at the center. Flatten slightly with your hand.

Then wet your hand and your clay, and begin pulling downward on the clay several times with index finger and thumb, turning the handle frequently so that you are pulling alternating sides. This is done so that the handle is even on both sides.

You will want to make sure to add water as you go. The clay should not be tugging against your hand as you pull.

Consistent pressure in your hand will create the most consistent handle.

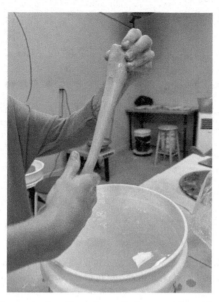

To thin out the handle, make an indent on either side of the center line on the same side, by running your thumb down along one side, and then the other. You can do this a few times. Making the edges a bit thinner gives your handle a more elegant look.

Bend the hand and measure it against the form you would like to attach it to, noting if it is a good size, thickness and consistency. It could be helpful to make a few handles per piece to have multiple options to choose from.

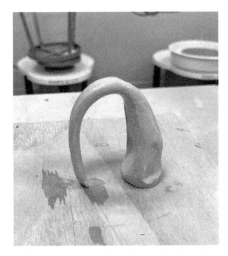

Once done, hang it over the edge of a wooden board or tile , so it can dry a bit on both sides and hold the curvature, before you attach it.

PULLING ON THE CYLINDER

Cut a piece of clay for your handle, and roll into a log shape; then, score, slip and attach at the top of your vessel. Allow this to dry for around 15 minutes, to give the attachment area a chance to dry and firm up somewhat.

Turn the mug (or other vessel) so that the handle is pointing down toward the floor, taking care to hold it gently. Wet your hand, then start at the top attachment point, and gently squeeze the handle allowing your hand to glide straight down towards the floor, and off. Avoid changing the angle of the mug, as this can cause a weakness in the top curve of the handle. Keep pulling until the handle reaches the required length, and is even on all sides—you want to get rid of any lumpiness.

Carefully arch the handle, and let it rest right above where it will be attached. If it is too long you can use your needle tool to cut a piece off at the bottom before attaching it. Score and slip the vessel and the bottom of the handle and attach, supporting the area from the inside with your other hand as you do so. Then, clean up any score marks or excess slip around the attachment areas with a paintbrush.

If some of the curve seems to have been lost in the attachment process, you can readjust the shape by gliding a moistened finger or paint brush handle on the inside of the handle to restore the curve.

Cover the vessel lightly with plastic to encourage it to dry slowly, and prevent it from cracking or separating at the seam. Bear in mind that you shouldn't try to pick up the mug by the handle until after its first firing!

For a larger pot like a pitcher, you might want to try making a double handle. Form a coil, then pull it extra long, fold over, and press together. Pull the handle a bit longer, compressing the two pieces together. Mark off the attachment points on the pitcher and measure the handle to the right length. Cut off the extra clay and round out the cut edges by patting with your finger.

Score, slip, and attach the handle, starting with the upper attachment point. Check that the handle is directly opposite the spout. To shape, push and lift slightly from the outside, and then smooth out the inside with your finger. Clean up the attachment points with a paintbrush dipped in water. To redefine the seam between the two layers, use a rubber-tipped tool with a beveled edge, and trace along the seam.

ATTACHING THE HANDLE

Use a knife tool to cut your handle to the exact right length.
Some potters will tap the cut end slightly with one finger to
open the clay slightly before adding slip.

Score the handle and the pot at the point where it will be attached.

Use a small amount of slip on the scored points

*Measure where the handle will go on the body of the form and
score the area where the handle will connect.*

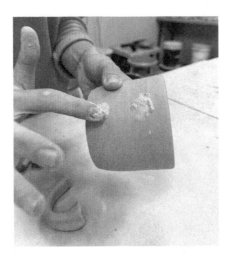

Add slip to the scored arms on the mug as well.

then carefully attach the handle, using gentle pressure from the inside of the mug to support the wall.

Smooth the edges around the attached points with your finger, using a little water, to seal the two pieces together. The aim should be to make the wall of the form and the handle look like a cohesive piece, as if the handle was pulled from the wall of the form.

Mark your initials or signature on the base of the form with a needle tool or stamp and then set aside and allow to dry completely.

INCISING AND DECORATING HANDLES

There are many options with decorating handles. You can make a wide range of accents to attach on to a form which can add a lot of personality to your piece and make it come alive.

The important thing to note is you do not want the handle to become too heavy in comparison to the body of the form. For example, if on a mug, the handle is too heavy, the form will likely tip. You also want to make sure to effectively attach the accents by using the slip and score technique. After the body of the form is thrown on the wheel you can get really creative with the piece, making more conceptual forms or adding patterns and textures with stamps.

You could also experiment with making your own decorating tools by cutting a profile into one end of an old credit card, or other stiff plastic, using an Exacto knife and use it to add a bit of flare to your form.

9

THROWING JARS

There are several ways to make a lidded jar, and in this chapter we will cover two open forms and one closed form. The closed form technique is a kind of 'cheat' method, whereby we can make both the lid and jar from a closed cylinder, simply cutting off the top section to make the lid. When making a lidded jar, it's important to make the jar and the lid at the same time, so they shrink at relatively the same rate and fit well together.

Making a lid is not as difficult as it might at first appear. Have a set of calipers on hand so that you can take accurate measurements. When starting out with making lidded jars, it's best to make two or three lids, so you'll have one that fits the intended jar best.

LIDDED JAR WITH GALLERY AND FLANGE ON VESSEL

The first few steps are always the same. Center the piece.

Open the base and compress the bottom.

And then begin pulling the wall.

The main thing to note is while you pull up the walls of your cylinder, you will want to release the pressure as you reach the top, so that the top will be a bit thicker, and you can make a shelf to sit the lid on.

To create the shelf, with the wheel spinning, position the edge of the wooden tool in the mid-section of the top of the cylinder, marking it slightly. You can use either a wooden knife tool or I use the edge of my pinky nail, as long as it has a nice sharp angle it can be used. Place the edge of the tool, or your pinky nail, on the middle of the rim. Gently push down the inner half of the rim. The clay will start to form a leg for your lid to later sit upon.

Using calipers, take the measurement from the outside edge of the gallery; i.e., the edges of the actual jar, not the inside of the gallery.

U p next, you will prepare a smaller amount of clay for the lid.

You will want to throw the lid in conjunction with the body of the jar. This will allow you to have proper measurements. Start by wedging a small amount of clay.

Center it and then flatten it down to make a disk on the wheel.

Use your calipers to measure the lid and cut to size. It's
important to get the measurements correct to ensure the vessel
will be airtight. An easy way to do this is to tilt one end of the
calipers downward, so that it scores the top of the lid, and then
use your needle tool to cut off the excess.

Note that the inward-facing prong of the calipers is used to measure the outside of the lid, and the outward-facing prong measures the inside of the lid.

To make a knob for the lid, get the wheel spinning again and push down with your finger halfway to the center of the disc, pushing in towards the center. Then, use your fingers to push the outer ring of the clay downward to form a gallery.

This will create a separation between the base of the lid, and the knob. As you push down, you will force the center of the disk upward, forming it into a knob.

To raise the beginning knob, using your thumbs, and one finger, begin collaring the clay, pinching the clay and raising it upwards.

The clay will naturally raise higher and form a more defined knob.

You will want to make sure that the form is shaped in a way where when it is glazed and smooth, your fingers will have a groove to hold on to. If it is a smooth knob, your fingers will have a hard time picking up the glass knob.

The final steps are adding definition to the lid, which will help with trimming later on.

As you complete the form, remeasure the base to try and have it as close as possible to fit inside the rim of the jar. You will also want to measure the top ledge of the lid to make sure that it can fit inside the gallery walls. This lid should sit inside the gallery, and on top of the shelf, not on top of the body of the form.

Cut the lid off the wheel using a wire tool. To check if the lid fits, push the needle tool into the base of the knob and lift slowly, placing it gently on the jar. Once you are happy with the fit, remove the lid, as you don't want it to fuse to the cylinder! Allow the two pieces to dry separately.

Once it's leather hard, you can trim off the top, using your needle tool at a downward angle to even out the clay, and then trim away the excess clay. Round off the top and add some definition around the edges.

THROWING THE LID UPSIDE DOWN FOR A GALLERY JAR

To throw an upside down lid for a gallery jar, you will want to approach the lid differently. You are essentially going to throw the base of the lid, rather than the top.

To begin, center and flatten the form. You will want to measure the outside of the lid so that it can sit inside of the gallery walls of the body, not on top of them.

Press down on the top of the form near the edge of the lid to start to add an indentation. Where you are pushing down will cause the clay to raise upwards.

*From there, take your left and right hand, pinching the clay
and pulling upwards, to begin raising a wall.*

*Measure the base to make sure it can fit inside of the gallery
rim of the jar's body.*

*And then measure the outer wall to make sure it can sit inside
of the shelf.*

Wire the lid of the bat and set it aside to dry. When the form is dry enough to trim you will want to make the knob.

To make a knob for the lid, use a small piece of clay, center it, and then push upward as if you are making a short cone. Then cinch in under the clay at the top with your fingers so that it mushrooms out. Fit your wire tool in the groove under the knob, cross the wire edges and pull. Then score and slip the underside of the knob and fit it to the lid.

JAR WITH CAP LID

A cap lid is one where the lid fits down over the edge of the jar. The aim is to create continuity in the lines, so that it will look as if the lid is a continuous part of the jar. This jar is essentially the opposite of the gallery jar, where the lid sits on the inside of the jar.

Use a rubber rib to create the belly of the jar and the shoulder, leaving a small section of the jar at the top cinched in so that the lid can fit snugly over it. Use the blunt end of the needle tool and run it over the outside of the top section, to create definition between the body of the jar and the flange, and to give the cap a place to sit.

Smooth out the flange using your fingers, then use the edge of the needle tool to angle the flange inward a bit, so the lid can slide down into place easily. If the flange is too high, you may need to trim some height off the top and round the edges of the flange again.

Use the inward facing prong side of the calipers to measure the widest area of the definition line, where the cap will sit on the outside of the jar.

To make the lid for the jar, throw a short cylinder, checking with the calipers to see how close you are to the size that you need. Widen it a bit if necessary, and if the lid is a bit too tall, you can trim some off using your needle tool, rounding off the edges. Then measure with the calipers again. To check if it fits, turn the lid still attached to the bat upside down and fit it over the vase.

Set aside to dry to leather hard, then turn the lid over on the wheel and secure with clay lugs. Trim the top to get rid of any excess clay and to give the lid some definition. Put some strips of newspaper over the rim of the jar, fit the lid, and set aside to dry. Letting them dry together encourages a good fit later.

ONE PIECE LIDDED JAR

The techniques covered so far have involved widening your basic cylinder form outwards, making a belly such as for a mug. Making a closed form requires learning how to make a section of the cylinder *narrower*, pushing the clay inwards using a technique called collaring, choking, or necking. Making a one-piece lidded jar is an example of how to use the closed form technique.

This jar will have a seat, or gallery, for the lid to rest on, while the lid will have a flange that rests on the gallery. The success of this form depends on making the sides of the jar straight, as the flange will not fit otherwise.

Start by placing the clay on the wheel, center and open the clay, and set the diameter for the jar, measuring with your calipers isn't necessary for this form.

Check the bottom for thickness and don't forget to compress the base with a sponge. You should leave at least half an inch for the foot of the jar.

Pull up the walls of the cylinder. Once you have the correct height you are aiming for you are ready to begin collaring in the top section of the cylinder.

Making a circle with your fingers and thumbs in a way that allows you to bring your hands closer together, thereby making the circle gradually smaller. Place your hands on either side of the cylinder with your thumbs touching at the front, and squeeze the top of the cylinder gently with your thumbs and forefingers. Some potters call this the "C position."

*After you collar, you can start to pull the wall, staring from the
collared area at the top, and bringing the clay in towards the
center.*

*Repeat the collaring motion, and check that your fingertips are
moving upwards as you close the form, so that the pressure is
moving up towards the rim and not towards the pot. By using
even pressure and moving your hands slowly upwards, this
forces the clay inwards and upwards.*

Close the form slowly so that the inside doesn't get twisted. When the top is almost closed, straighten the sides of the jar using a straight rib. Use your needle tool to cut off any excess clay at the top, then use a wooden tool pressed lightly into the top to close it off completely. Once the top is completely closed, run the wooden tool over the top to smooth it out.

Now prepare to make the flange for the jar. With the wheel spinning, use either a flat wooden tool or chop stick to create a groove at the point where the curve meets the straight side of the jar.

Using the blunt end of the needle tool or chop stick, press in halfway to create the flange, being sure to use water to eliminate any friction.

Trim the base with your wooden tool and then cut the jar from the wheel, set aside and allow it to dry until leather hard and ready for further trimming

Use the needle tool to poke a small hole in the flange to allow trapped air to be released from the inside of the form while it dries, and to prevent cracking.

TRIMMING ONE PIECE LIDDED JAR

*Place the jar back on the wheel, and angle the needle tool
against the groove you cut earlier, slowly cutting into the
flange. Keeping your hands steady, allow the needle tool to cut
through the bottom of the flange until the top is released.*

*Now you can use your trimming tool to clean up the edges of
the bottom of the jar. Place the lid upside down on top of the jar
to trim the rim of the top as well. Bevel the lid so it will sit
better on the jar bottom, and trim away any excess from the
inside of the jar to ensure a tight fit with the lid.*

Finish the piece by placing the lid right side up and fitting it snuggly on top of the form. Trim away any excess on the outside.

An optional step is to mold or hand-build a small knob for the lid, and attach it so that it's easy to remove the lid.

10
TEA POTS

aking a teapot builds on the knowledge you have accumulated so far, being how to make a lidded jar, and how to make and attach a handle. The only additional skill introduced in the making of a teapot is the making of a spout. This will be attached in the same way as a handle. For a refresher on throwing a jar, refer to the previous chapter.

THROWING THE BODY OF THE TEA POT

Before you begin, make sure you have portioned out the clay for the teapot, lid, spout, and handle. Make the body of the teapot and lid first, as these will take two or three days to dry, while the spout and handle will dry within one or two hours. Remember, you don't want any of the pieces drying out much more than the others, to avoid uneven rates of shrinkage. Make all the pieces and allow them to dry sufficiently, before assembling your teapot.

Start by making a basic jar, then measure the inside of the pot with your calipers, and make a gallery for the lid in the same way as for the lidded jar.

Next, make the lid. Measure the diameter of the lid with your calipers to be sure it will fit, and trim away any excess if necessary.

MAKING THE SPOUT

To make the spout, center a small piece of clay

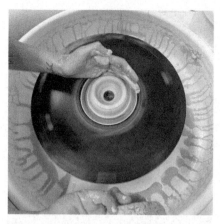

Next, open the clay, pushing down all the way to the wheel head. Here you can play around with the design, depending on what you would like the spout to look like.

Then raise a narrow cylinder. With your finger on the inside of the cylinder, push out the bottom section, making it a bit wider than the top.

Next, collar in the top section so that it is narrower than the bottom. Or, you can collar in the mid-section, so that it's narrower than the top or bottom.

If you want to lengthen the spout a bit more, but it is too narrow for your finger to fit inside, you can use the blunt end of your pin tool inserted into the opening, and pull the spout up slightly as if you are raising the wall with your fingers.

Trim any excess at the base with your wooden trimming tool.

Once you have the desired size, you will want to angle to spout to help give it a natural curve. Using the needle tool, pull the spout away from the center to curve it.

Allow the spout to dry somewhat before removing it from the wheel, to make sure that it doesn't lose its shape.

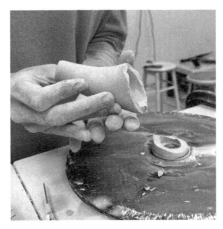

Allow to dry somewhat, and then cut off the spout at an angle
from the bat, angling your wire tool downwards towards you.
Alternatively, you will need to cut off a section of the spout at
an angle later, so that it angles upwards on the pot. You can
always cut away a bit more later, or adjust the angle slightly.

Cutting the spout at exactly the right angle can be a challenge when you are starting out. It's best to throw several spouts for each teapot, so that you have more than one option to choose from. For best results, it's recommended to attach the spout when it's soft leather hard, as it will still be pliable enough for the edge to be molded to fit the pot.

MAKING THE HANDLE

When attaching this kind of handle, put your hand on the inside of the pot at the point where you are attaching the handle, and push outwards slightly to avoid deforming the pot.

Some potters feel that scoring is unnecessary for

attaching spouts and handles, and that using slip is enough. However, scoring the attachment areas creates a bit more surface area for the clay to join to. As a beginner, you may want to always include this step, to be sure that your attachments don't come off later.

PIECING IT ALL TOGETHER

After trimming the lid to fit the body of the tea pot, poke a hole through the top to allow air flow when pouring tea. This will hinder any sputtering to happen, and will aid in a smoother pour.

Next, pull a handle for the pot, leaving to dry for about twenty minutes. Cut the handle to your desired size and measure it against the body. Check that the handle has a good curve.

Score both the handle and body of the pot.

And then add slip, which will act similar to glue.

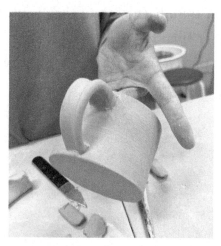

Attach the handle, and smooth out the edges. The handle should look as if it is part of the form, and not just sitting on top of the body.

Next, we will attach the spout.

The best place to place your spout is on the shoulder of the pot. As a rule of thumb, the top of the spout should be level or slightly higher than the top of the tea pot. You also want to make sure that it is positioned directly opposite the handle.

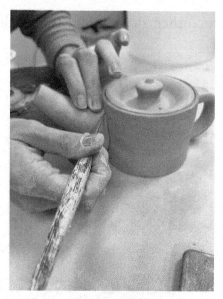

*Position the spout on the pot and trace around the edges with
your potter's knife or needle tool to mark out the position.*

*Make sure not to press all the way through the body. The goal is
just to create a visual of where it will be attached.*

Now you will need to cut a round hole in one side of the
teapot, or you may want to cut a series of smaller holes,
creating a filter. If you don't have a hole-making tool, a

potter's knife, or other sharp knife tool, will work just as well.

To create straining holes or a filter, use the needle tool to poke holes into the body, making sure to stay within the outlined area where the spout will be attached.

Smooth out the holes on the inside and outside, and go over them again. It will be very hard to touch this up once the spout is attached, so make sure you have it up to your standard.

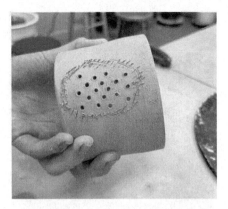

*Next, score along the outlined area as well as score the edge of
the spout that will be attached to the body.*

Add slip

And attach, smoothing the edges to make a seamless seal.

One way to prepare for attaching the spout is to let it stand in a centimeter of water for a few minutes, to soften up slightly before attaching. When the base of the spout has softened, apply a small amount of slip to the pot and attach the spout so that it angles upwards. The top of the spout will be firm enough for you to apply some pressure without deforming. Alternatively, score and slip the pot where you will attach the spout.

TIPS FOR BETTER POURING

Some teapots can be a disappointment in that while they look very pretty, they don't pour very well; they're either too fast, too slow, or get choked with air.

There are some ways around this, and to encourage your teapots to pour well. Depending on the kind of spout you have made, one way is to create a small air pocket by pushing out the bottom section of the spout slightly with your finger just before attaching it, creating a small outward bulge.

You can also encourage good flow by creating a small channel in the spout. Run the blunt end of your needle tool back and forth along the inside of the spout a few times.

Another tip, and the simplest way according to seasoned potters (and tea drinkers) is to poke a hole in the lid with your needle tool—this will allow air into the teapot while pouring.

Once leather hard, put the pot upside down on the wheel and attach it with clay lugs to trim the bottom. Then turn the pot over, fit the lid, and trim away any excess clay from the lid.

11

THROWING VASES, BOTTLES, AND PITCHERS

The process for throwing vessels such as vases, bottles, and pitchers is essentially the same, with a few minor adaptations. All of these forms start with a basic cylinder, but vases and bottles will have a narrower neck, while a pitcher has a modified rim to create the spout, and a handle attached.

MAKING A VASE

To begin making your cylinder, start by centering and opening the clay,

As you open the form, take care to create a good curve on the inside, and removing any excess clay from the base of the cylinder. This creates a trench for you to hold on to as you pull up the walls.

*Be mindful of the narrower opening you are aiming for when
throwing these forms. Avoid letting the opening get larger as
you go; try to keep it tapered inward as you're raising the walls.
When the cylinder is at the desired height, smooth out the rim
by letting it run through your fingers, and compress slightly
with your sponge.*

Before you start to shape the top inwards, remove all the
excess water from the vessel while you can still get your
hand to the bottom. Using your sponge to do this, you can
also push out the bottom of the clay somewhat to give your
bottle some volume. Be sure to thin out the walls before you
begin shaping the vessel.

*Now you can begin collaring the top, wetting your hands
slightly before you do so. You want to avoid putting too much
pressure on the neck of the vessel to begin with, as you don't
want any part of the vessel to be thinner or narrower than the
rim.*

*First, bring the top of the vessel in slightly before bringing the
neck in, to prevent the clay from buckling. Bring your hands
right up to the rim and squeeze directly on it, to get the rim
pointed in the direction that you want the pot to go.*

The metal rib can help with the curvature of the vessel, to smooth out the slope.

To bellow out the rim, use one hand on the outside of the form and gently guide it in towards the center, while the other hand pulls the rim away from the middle.

M aintain an even pressure with your hands, and keep an eye on the opening of the vessel as you go, so that it doesn't warp out of shape. At this point you will have a basic vase shape.

MAKING A BOTTLE

To turn your form into a bottle, you will want to create shoulders and lengthen the neck area. Shoulders can be a hard form to achieve, but with practice it is achievable.

Begin with the first step of centering.

Open and compress the form.

And then raise the walls. You want to aim for a lot of height with this piece, and you will want to make the cylinder higher that you would image. You will want to make sure that you are satisfied with the walls of your form before moving on to creating the shoulders and narrowing the opening of the form. Take any water out of the middle so that there is not a puddle forming on the inside that will be hard to get out as the form progresses.

Next, make the shoulders. You can begin by collaring the form at the top, where you would like the neck to begin. It's normal for the rim to undulate slightly at this point. If this happens, compress the rim slightly with your thumb and middle finger, without putting any pressure on it, but just letting it slide through your fingers.

As you collar you will want to raise the walls to build height. To create the neck you will switch between collaring and raising the walls.

After you collar, you will have a thicker rim to work with and you can begin raising the walls from the end of the shoulders to the top of the vessel. Depending on how long you would like the neck of your bottle to be, you can lengthen it by pulling up the walls slightly and collaring again. If the neck is taller than you need, cut off some of the height with your needle tool and compact the rim again.

Make sure the neck is small enough for your intended cork or stopper to fit into, keep in mind the drying rate of the clay if intending to use a cork or stopper later on. Since collaring narrows the vessel, this thickens the wall and requires pulling up to thin it out again.

With a flexed metal rib, start at the bottom of the cylinder. Slowly move your hands up to the top, shaving off the loose clay and slip, and firming up the vessel. This is especially important when you are making a rounded vessel with a pronounced shoulder at the top, so that it's strong enough, and won't collapse later. Once you are happy with the shape, run over the shoulders with a flexible metal rib tool to compress them again and soften the curve, and also to add definition between the neck and the walls.

Put any finishing touches on the piece and then wire off and set aside to dry for trimming.

A seasoned potter's trick to add some buoyancy and volume to your bottle is to seal your lips, place them over the neck of the bottle, and then blow gently into it. However, you don't have to do this if you feel squeamish about putting your mouth on the clay!

MAKING A PITCHER

The challenge of making a functional pitcher is that it needs to be large enough to hold a decent amount of liquid, yet also light enough to use comfortably. It needs to be lightweight so that it's not cumbersome to use, but not so light that it breaks easily.

Start by throwing a tall, narrow cylinder. Swell out the belly and neck areas, adding fullness to the form, especially in the lower section.

The metal rib can help with bellowing out the form and creating a soft curve in the body. While using the metal rib on the outside of the piece, press into the wall on the inside of the form, pushing against where the rib is gliding against. Pull a wall with the rib to help shape the vessel.

When you are happy with the shape, the last step is adding the spout. Wet your hands, and use your thumb and forefinger to pinch about a quarter of the rim's circumference. While you pinch with one hand, take the pointer finger of your other hand and pull the clay into the pinched area. As you pull upward gently with your fingers, thin and sharpen the rim.

Creating a thinner edge allows for better pouring; if the edge is too rounded, then the pitcher will tend to dribble. When the spout area has been thinned and shaped, pinch in an indentation on either side of the spout to create a channel and accentuate the spout.

Pull a long tapered handle and let it dry for a short while. When the body of the pitcher is dry enough to attach the handle, make sure not to attach it too near the top, as this isn't conducive to holding with comfort when the pitcher is full.

12

THROWING PLATES

Becoming proficient at throwing plates takes a bit more practice than throwing a bowl or a cup. When making flatware such as plates or platters, the clay doesn't need to be as firm as when you are throwing taller vessels. Since you will be pushing a large amount of clay outward, it helps to use a softer clay, as it will be much more difficult to flatten down a firm piece of clay. You will also need to use a bat when throwing a plate, as a flat piece is much more likely to stretch and deform when you remove it from the wheel.

Some potters also use a clay bat to act as a stabilizer for the throwing bat. This is a thin pad of clay thrown onto the wheel, scraped clean of slip, and then dried to leather hard with a heat gun. The bat can then be lightly trimmed to make sure that it's perfectly flat.

Weigh out around four pounds of clay for a dinner-sized plate, or one and a half pounds for a side plate. Begin by getting the wheel spinning at a medium to medium-high speed. Start by centering the clay, coning up and down.

After centering your clay, use either the outside edge of your hand in the karate chop position, or your fist, and press down with the other hand, keeping your hands steady.

Flatten down the clay with your right hand until you have a wide flat disc. You want to make sure that it's flat on the top, and even on the sides. Holding a sponge in your fist as you widen the form can help you apply water as you throw, especially for large plates.

Depending on how large of a plate you are throwing, as the clay disk expands outwards, it will make contact with your forearm, so you may need to stop the wheel and wet your arm some more, to prevent the clay from dragging on dry skin.

If the edge is somewhat uneven, use your wooden knife tool to cut off the edge and remove the ring of clay. Measure the base of the plate; it should be around a half to three quarters of an inch thick.

Flatten the inside using a rib tool or a sponge, starting from the outside, and moving slowly towards the middle. Compressing the bottom is very important to compact the platelets, so that the clay binds together well. You can also use a metal rib, flexing down on the clay body to smooth it out and erase any marks.

To begin making the rim of the plate, slow the wheel speed down, and push in under the edge of the plate using your thumb. Keep the fleshy part of your thumb against the bat, and use the nail up against the clay, stabilizing your hand with the other hand. You could also push on the outer edge of the plate with your sponge; this will force the clay upwards.

Then pull this section up into a small wall, so you now have a wide cylinder.

Now wet your fingers and push out on the edge of the wall, until it forms the rim of the plate. Using a plastic rib, sponge, or your fingers, push into the wall to flatten it into a rim. Using a flexible metal rib, smooth out the section between the rim and the bottom of the plate, checking that it has a good curvature to support the rim.

Cut the plate from the bat, but leave it on the bat to dry to leather hard. Since plates are generally thicker than other pieces, they usually take a day longer to dry. Turning them over promotes even drying. However, you need to take extra care when turning them, so that they don't get warped. You want to keep them as flat as possible for the entire time. It's recommended to turn them using a wooden bat on either side.

13
TRIMMING

Once your completed piece has dried to leather hard, it's time to trim off any unwanted clay, and smooth over the surfaces. This is the primary reason for trimming greenware. In fact, a piece that has picked up a lot of throw marks or uneven sections during throwing can be radically improved by trimming it well.

Another reason for trimming is to delineate the piece from its base, which can also create a line for decoration on your vessel; for example, around the foot ring. This demarcation also creates a collection point for glaze, and provides a place for the glaze to stop running.

Your pot should be leather hard when you begin trimming. Some potters have likened the consistency to cutting through cheddar cheese, and for this reason the leather hard stage is also sometimes called "cheese hard." If you can hear the pot humming when you trim it, it's probably a bit too dry. Don't attempt trimming if the clay is still soft, as this will clog up your tools.

First, you will need to center the piece on the wheel. Use the concentric rings on the wheel to help you center your pot. If you are using a bat, it needs to be smooth. and should be dampened slightly before trimming.

CENTERING YOUR POT FOR TRIMMING

There are a few different methods for centering the pot on the wheel. Get the wheel spinning slowly, place your bowl rim-side down onto the wheel, and hold your index finger against the foot.

*Where the pot touches your finger, this indicates that the pot is
slightly off-center. Move your piece slightly in the direction
your finger is pointing, repeating until your finger makes
constant contact with the pot as it spins*

Another method is to tap the pot consistently as it spins, tapping at a constant rate. Your left hand should be on the opposite side of the pot, not stopping the movement, but just allowing it to glide past your fingers gently.

You could also use a method called placing; stop the wheel when the pot touches your thumbs, and then push it away from you, repeating that process until the pot is in the center. Or, you could try bumping the piece lightly with your thumbs, bracing the pot with your fingers around the other side

To secure the piece to the wheel while you trim, use scraps of fresh clay, and make three-four clay coils or lugs. Hold the pot with one hand, then use your thumb to press the clay lugs against the wheel head around the edges of the pot, to fix it in place.

Try to position these at equal distances from each other. Fixing the pot down with lugs makes the trimming process much easier for beginner potters.

If you want to do any trimming on the inside, this has to be done first. Once you have trimmed the foot ring, the bowl will be too fragile to make any changes to the inside. In this case, you will have to fix it down with clay lugs, with the base on the wheel first.

To smooth the inside of the bowl, soften the walls with a sponge to dampen the clay. Then use a rubber rib to burnish the surface, starting at the center, and moving all the way up to the top.

TRIMMING THE WALLS

*Most beginner tool kits should have a bird-head trimming tool,
and a double-headed loop tool. We'll use the loop tool to take off
most of the excess clay from the outside of the pot.*

*Start with the round side of the double-headed tool, holding it
as an extension of your finger, pressing the end down into the
palm of your hand. Make sure that enough of the loop is
protruding, so the clay can come off easily.*

At this point your pot will be noticeably thicker in the base
and lower sections of the walls. You will want to trim away
excess clay so that the walls are more-or-less even
throughout the entire pot. The curve of the bowl will
continue as one uninterrupted curve, with the foot ring

simply intercepting that curve.

Steady the pot with the fingers of your left hand on top of the pot. Beginner potters will often try to trim with the wheel spinning a bit too slowly. This is largely a matter of gaining confidence in trimming, and learning to be strong in your movements. Also, always use sharp tools, as you will have to use more pressure if your tools are blunt. Using extra force could create undulations in the walls, deform the pot, or puncture the walls or the base.

You want the wheel to be spinning fast enough so that the pieces fly off, and don't just fall onto the wheel. Spinning the wheel faster also helps you cut through the clay more evenly, and gives a more consistent form. If you are trimming more slowly, you might want to gather the pieces that you trim off in your hand as you go, rather than letting them land all over the wheel head, where they will get in the way.

Use a trimming tool to remove excess material, taking care not to remove too much in any one movement. When you are happy with the shape of the walls, use a soft rubber rib to press the grog exposed by trimming back under the surface; this smooths out the surface. Then you can use a flexible metal rib against the side of the pot, flexed at a slight angle to even out the surface even more. Using the flat part of the rib contoured to the surface of the pot will burnish the surface, and remove any remaining trimming rings.

After the excess clay on the walls has been removed, you can begin to define the foot ring itself. The foot ring will divide the bowl into two distinct sections; the foot and the walls.

TRIMMING THE FOOT RING

Get the wheel spinning at a medium speed. Hold the trimming tool in your right hand, steadying the pot with your left hand. Angle the trimming tool in to trim the height and width of the foot ring.

Use calipers and a potter's needle to score a line that will mark the outside diameter of the foot ring. It should be around a quarter inch wide for a medium-sized bowl.

If the bottom is very wide, it may hang over the belly of the bowl; in this case it is definitely too wide, and you will need to trim off a fair amount to make it smaller. This might leave a substantial edge from the bowl to the foot; trim that away as well to smooth out this connecting area between the foot ring and the body of the bowl. Once that section is as wide as you want it, use the broad edge of the tool to round out the area just below the foot.

Gently push the pointed end down through the clay, starting either in the middle working outwards, or from the inside of the foot ring working towards the center. Beginning in the center decreases the weight that is pressing down on the center of the bowl, reducing the chances that the bowl will get too thin and collapse.

A s you trim away the center, press down periodically on the clay in the center; you want to be sure it doesn't have any give, as that would mean it's too thin, and you are in danger of cutting through the floor of the bowl.

When the bulk of the clay has been trimmed away, switch to a smaller tool to smooth out the surface even further. A smaller tool with a more severe angle allows you to cut right up close to the foot ring, without fear of cutting away too much.

An important last step is to check that the middle point at the base of the pot is lower than the foot ring. Place the flat end of your flexible metal rib over the foot ring. If it touches in the middle, you need to trim down the middle a bit more, otherwise the bowl will spin.

As you become more experienced at trimming, you will get better at judging whether you have trimmed away the right amount at the base. There are a few methods you can use to check. One way is to tap the clay on the bottom; if it's too thin, it will sound hollow. The tone when you tap the bottom should match that of the walls of the piece.

You can also check the weight in your hands; your pot should feel well-balanced. If the bottom feels heavy, you may need to trim away a little more. This technique will become easier with practice, as you are better able to gauge the feel of your pieces.

Now you can sign your name on the underside of the pot if you wish!

TRIMMING A TUMBLER

Trimming a tumbler requires a different approach to trimming. In this instance you have to keep a tall pot steady as your trim, and you have a smaller surface to trim.

Instead of using clay lugs, you can throw a simple clay chuck to hold the pot in place. Chucks can either be wet-clay or bisque-fired forms, and are used to hold an inverted pot in place for trimming. In this instance, center a handful of stiffer clay on to the bat, roughly the diameter of the rim of the tumbler. Put the tumbler on top of the clay, and make any necessary adjustments so that the tumbler fits snugly. Once it's centered, press the tumbler firmly onto the bat.

Where a bowl has a curved floor, a tumbler will have a flat floor to match the squared-off edges of the walls. Using a smaller trim tool, trim away in the same way as before, making sure to keep both hands on the tool, as this increases your accuracy. Then trim the outside, and burnish in the same way as for the bowl. When you're happy with the tumbler, remove it from the clay chuck, and clean up the rim with a damp sponge.

TRIMMING WITH A CHUCK

Trimming a form with a narrow neck or uneven rim—such as a bottle or a pitcher— presents an extra challenge, since these forms can't be placed upside down on the wheel without some kind of support. One solution for this is to use one or more clay chucks. These are bisque-fired clay cylinders, open on each end, that can be used to support a bottle or vase during trimming. They can also be used for trimming pots if you wish. You can make a variety of chucks in different shapes and sizes, with sides that are straight, or slant inward or outward. They can also be stacked on top of each other if need be, if the neck of your piece is very long.

For trimming a jug or pitcher, you would use a reverse chuck that the jug or pitcher will fit over, rather than into. Making the chuck with sides that slant outwards slightly will mean that you can use the chuck for jugs of varying sizes.

Using a chuck has some pros and cons, and while some potters swear by them, others may find them cumbersome for regular use. Trimming with a chuck has a different feel to it, since the piece being trimmed is more elevated. The clay of the vessel being trimmed must be leather hard; if it's too wet it might stick, and if too dry the piece could pop off while you are trimming. The chuck could also leave a mark on the walls of the pot. This can usually be cleaned up quite easily with a sponge or rib. Clean up marks inside a deep or narrow vessel using a sponge on a stick.

Among the advantages of using a chuck; you can dispense with the use of clay lugs on your pots, which can distort the form or damage the surface. Initially, however, you may want to keep using lugs on the chuck to make sure it stays in place. It also allows you to trim pots that are not entirely level, and it reduces the chances of cracking or damage by taking pressure off the rim of the pot. Chucks are perfect for trimming lidded jars, since there is no disruption to the flange.

MAKING A CHUCK

It's recommended that you throw a chuck as a simple cylinder, much as if you were making a spout. Make sure that it has a low base to provide stability, and with either a narrow neck, or a neck that is slightly wider than the base. Trim the base to remove any sharp edges. You may want to make a variety of chucks to suit different purposes, including some with a long neck for trimming narrow forms. When the chuck is bone-dry, bisque-fire it, and then store in a bucket of water, as it has to be saturated when you use it.

14

DECORATIVE TECHNIQUES

SLIP TRAILING

Slip trailing is a decorative technique for pottery that involves applying slip, or liquified clay, onto clay pieces in lines or patterns. The slip can be applied using a variety of applicators, and these can either be commercially bought, or made at home by repurposing cake decorators, squeeze bottles, or other containers with a pointed tip.

After the bisque has been fired, the slip trails create a raised texture that can add complexity and tactile elements to a piece. By adding colored stains or metal oxides to the slip, you can create striking and colorful designs on your ceramic pieces. Slip will fuse to the clay body when fired, so it won't rub or flake off.

Slip can be applied to pottery that is leather hard, bone-dry, or still in a workable stage. It can also be used on bisqueware, but this is trickier, due to the different shrinkage rates of the slip and the bisque piece.

To make slip to use for slip trailing, soak dried scraps of clay in water until it's slaked down into a slurry. You could also use slurry from your reclaim bucket (assuming it is the same clay that you used for the body of the piece you want to decorate). Slip is technically thinner than slurry, so you may need to add water to get the right consistency. If you use different types of clay for your pieces, it's best to have separate slip containers, so you can maintain the consistency of your ceramic pieces.

Use a fine sieve (at least an 80 mesh) to remove lumps and grog, so that the texture is consistent and smooth.

You can also make slip by breaking up bone-dry clay sealed in a bag. Break up the clay using a mallet, and then a rolling pin, until you have a fine powder. Pour this into a container, add water, and mix up using a handheld blender. The consistency should resemble sour cream or yogurt. Now put this through a sieve or strainer to remove any lumps. Tapping the strainer against the bowl you are straining into, will allow the slip to go through quite quickly.

Now you are ready to add in your colorant. Add one ounce of powdered Mason stain to ten ounces of slip (two tablespoons equals one ounce). Be sure to level off the spoon and wear your dust mask while adding the Mason stain. Mix in thoroughly with a spatula and then with your handheld blender. Now put the slip through the strainer again. Store in an airtight container, or a resealable plastic bag for future use.

Slip can now be applied to your pottery using trailing applicators of various types and sizes. You can achieve different effects using squeeze bottles, applicator bulbs, and different tip sizes. You can also apply the slip using a paint brush.

An applicator bulb has a threaded opening that can be fitted with different tip sizes. A syringe applicator can be used to create extra fine trails, and provides exceptional control, accuracy, and consistent thickness. A squeeze applicator is used to create more prominent design elements.

To fill the applicator, squeeze the bottle and insert the tip into your container of slip. As you release the pressure from your fingers, the slip will be drawn into the container.

To apply slip to a piece, shake the slip down towards the tip, tilt the applicator to one side, and squeeze gently. Be sure to move the tip away from the open end so that the slip trails out behind the applicator.

You may want to practice with different applicators on a slab of leather hard clay to get a feel for the technique, how much pressure to use, and keeping your hand steady so that you are creating smooth lines. If the applicator feels awkward in your hand, try one of a different size until you find one that feels comfortable and natural in your hand.

Once you are ready to try slip-trailing on a finished piece, start by drawing out a design that you have in mind. If you are not happy with the result, you can wipe it off with a sponge. If you've already bisque-fired the piece with the slip applied, you can remove it by sanding it off. (Remember to wear a dust mask whenever you are sanding.)

SGRAFFITO

Sgraffito is an ancient pottery-decorating technique that involves applying layers of color, either underglazes or slips to leather hard pottery, then scratching off parts of the layers to reveal the clay color underneath. This technique can be used to add contrasting patterns, images and textures to pieces. The word sgraffito comes from Italian, and means "to scratch."

The roots of sgraffito can be traced back to the Italian Renaissance, when it was widely employed to decorate building facades. It also gained popularity in the Middle East, and has been found in African art.

Tools that can be used to employ this technique include a wire stylus, small ribbon- sculpting tools, needle and wire tools, and a rubber scraper for tidying up around the designs. The tools you use to create your designs depend on the kind of effect you want to produce. To create a more textured surface, use more pointed tools, and apply more pressure.

Select or sketch out a design, then transfer this to a piece of tracing paper, and trace onto the clay by making indentations with a sharp pencil. Then apply two to three coats of underglaze of slip, applying each coat in an alternate direction. You can either paint the whole piece, or only paint on a design. Leave to dry for a day before starting to scratch off.

When the piece is dry, you can begin scratching patterns into the design, or scratch off the paint around the design. Use a soft, dry brush to remove clay debris as you work. Scoring parallel lines is a typical method employed to create shaded areas.

After bisque-firing your piece, you can touch up the underglaze or slip where needed and allow it to dry, then apply your clear glaze before glaze firing.

RELIEF CARVING

Carving designs into your ceramic pieces is another way to add complexity, exercise your creativity, and have fun while you're doing it.

Your piece should be firm leather hard when carving, as this allows your tool to cut through easily without gouging. If you work from a sketch, begin by dividing up your space by drawing guidelines on the piece that segment the space into quarters or thirds. Consider which areas of the form you will carve, then lightly trace out your design using a sharp pencil.

You can carve using a pencil, porcupine quill, ball stylus tool, or sgraffito tool. Angle your tool at a shallow angle to create clean lines. With your hand inside the pot, apply gentle counter-pressure to keep track of the amount of force you are using, and the moisture content of the clay.

Try using a variety of shallow, deep, and intermediate angles as you carve—small changes in the angle of your strokes can create a sense of volume and depth. The first lines will form the skeleton of your design. Using directional lines can help to define the flow of a pattern. If you want to separate an object from the background, carve out a gentle slope away from the most defining lines.

If you carve too deeply, you can easily repair the area by scoring it, applying some slip, and adding a bit of clay with the same moisture content to fill in the gap.

Allow crumbs of clay debris to dry a bit before brushing

them away; if you try to do this while the clay is still wet, they will clog up your carved lines.

Rehydrate your pot if it gets too dry by pouring water in and out of it, and pat or spray the surface with water. Repeat as necessary while carving, so that your clay is moist enough to allow you to carve into it easily.

You can add further dimension and interest to your piece by integrating raised or recessed dots into the surface to provide both visual and tactile focal points. Attach small pieces of clay to create raised dots or other shapes at the high points of your design. You can also include contrasting textures, with some smooth and some rough areas. Textures can either be static, or have a distinct directional flow.

Adding embellishments to hidden areas such as the flange or the bottom of the pot can add an element of surprise and discovery that will engage the viewer.

15

WHAT COMES NEXT? AN OVERVIEW OF GLAZING, FIRING, AND SELLING YOUR POTTERY

Once your pottery piece is completed and bone-dry, it's ready for the next stages of firing and glazing. You may plan to start a pottery business, or to display your work at fairs and galleries. This chapter aims to give a brief overview of these processes, which will be explored more fully in further publications.

BISQUE FIRING

Pottery is typically fired in two stages. Bisque firing is the first stage; this prepares the piece for further processes such as applying glazes. Glaze firing is the second stage; this is the stage at which glazes melt and fuse with the clay body.

The bisque firing process removes any residual moisture, and turns the pottery porous, which enables stains, glazes, and underglazes to adhere to the ceramic surface. It also increases the strength of the pottery, and reduces the chances of it cracking or collapsing during glaze firing. It's essential to check that you use the correct firing temperature for your clay and glazes.

Bisque firing must be done under controlled heat conditions, with the kiln being heated and then cooled slowly. It can be done in an electric or fuel-burning kiln, but electric is preferable as it heats more slowly, and makes it easier to control the temperature.

The kiln should be set up with the bottom shelf at least one inch above the surface. Pottery ready for firing can be stacked together in the kiln and should be at least an inch away from the walls. The cover should be 1.5 to 2 inches away from the wares.

Clay firing ranges use the cone rating system; pyrometric cones are small ceramic tapers with different melting points, which are numbered according to the temperature at which they will bend and eventually collapse in the kiln.

A good setting for bisque firing is between cone 08 and 04 (with 04 being the hotter setting). The higher the temperature setting used, the less porous the ceramic becomes. Firing at cone 06 shrinks the clay and increases its porosity, enabling it to accept glazes easily. Firing at cone 04 improves the strength and durability of the pottery.

The firing ramp is the rate at which the kiln is heated and cooled and is measured in degrees per hour. The kiln needs to be heated up very slowly and turned up bit by bit, and this can take anywhere between three and eight hours, depending on the power of the kiln. Some potters will heat up the kiln overnight at a very low heat.

Once the ideal temperature has been reached, the kiln needs to be cooled down slowly. Expect the cooling time to be the same number of hours as it was for heating. A good rule of thumb is to allow it to cool overnight, before removing your pots from the kiln the next day.

It's technically possible to skip the bisque firing stage and go straight to glaze firing. However, this can lead to the ceramic cracking or falling apart, especially when using commercial glazes. The chemically bonded water and organic gases still present in the clay can also cause the glaze to bubble or develop pinholes, or not adhere properly.

Only highly experienced potters who mix their own glazes to be compatible with a single fire will skip the bisque firing step. Glazes used in single firing will often have a higher clay content.

GLAZING

Ceramic glazing is used to add color and texture to pottery and to give it a smooth, glass-like finish. Glaze also makes it possible for fired earthenware to hold liquid.

There are hundreds of different ways to glaze pottery, and the glazing process is a chance for the potter to give free reign to their creative expression on the blank canvas of the pot.

Glazes are composed primarily of silica, alumina, and flux. Of these, silica is the primary glass-forming ingredient that will form the glossy surface of the completed pot. Alumina gives the glaze some substance and viscosity, which helps it stay on the pottery, and flux helps to control the melting point of the glaze.

Some of the most common ways glazes are applied is by dipping, pouring, spraying, or brushing. It's always a good idea to test the glaze first on a small piece of tile to see how it will turn out. Also, be sure to check your pottery for any rough spots you may have missed before applying glazes and remove these with wet sandpaper.

Glazes must be properly mixed, sieved, and stirred again to get the right consistency. Different products will yield different consistencies, so be sure to follow the package directions carefully.

Dipping is one of the easiest methods of applying glaze, and is often used to establish a base layer before decorating the piece. Mix up the glaze in a bucket and use tongs to dip the piece. A thinner consistency is better for dipping.

The basic method for dipping is to grip the piece firmly but gently with the tongs and then lower slowly into the glaze. For a bowl or a mug, dip the piece in like a ladle, allowing the glaze to pour in and out of the vessel. Dip for three to five seconds and then remove. Shake the piece a little to get rid of any excess, dry the base, and then set it down. Use a soft brush or sponge to smooth over any drip marks or tong marks.

For pouring, fill a small cup or bowl with glaze, and first glaze the inside by pouring into and out of the vessel. Then pour over the outside of the piece, turning it as you pour to make sure the piece is covered on all sides.

For brushing on glaze, use soft brushes to avoid streaking. Large flat brushes are recommended for bigger pieces and small, round-tipped ones to make patterns. Try to cover an area with a single sweep. Allow to dry completely, and then go over again in another direction, applying two or three coats in total.

Spraying is another popular method of applying glazes. This is done with a spray gun and requires a banding wheel to rotate the pottery while it's being sprayed. Spraying can be used to apply entire layers, for decorating, and for creating interesting gradient effects.

Allow the first layer to dry completely before spraying a second time, checking that the glaze isn't too thick in any areas. Don't try to wipe wet glaze as it will smudge—rather smooth out any drips or thick areas with sandpaper later.

There are also a variety of decorative techniques that can be used after a base layer has been dipped, poured, or painted on with a brush. Dripping, splattering, or stippling with a brush, or trailing with an applicator, are all ways to add eye-catching details, colors, and textures.

Always make sure that glazes are completely dry before putting your pottery into the kiln. Any residual moisture can ruin the glaze or even cause the pottery to explode. The glaze will dry relatively quickly, since the bisque will draw out the water from the glaze, which leaves a powdery residue on the surface of the pot.

GLAZE FIRING

Different glazes are fired at different temperatures, as they need to reach a certain heat point to melt and bond properly to the ceramic. When selecting a pottery glaze, take care to select one that matches the firing temperature of your clay body. Glazes are categorized as low-fire, mid-fire, and high-fire in the same way as pottery clay.

Low fire glazes can produce strong color without needing as much power as higher fire glazes. Mid fire glazes tend to be quite strong, which makes them highly suitable for functional ware.

Once glaze has been applied to your bisqueware, it should be left to dry completely, then loaded carefully into the kiln. Pieces should not touch each other in the kiln as the glazes will melt together and fuse the pots together permanently. The kiln will again be heated slowly until it reaches the optimal temperature, and then cooled down slowly.

As the glaze heats up and starts to melt, it interacts with the underlying clay layer. Bonding between the bisque and glaze happens best when both the clay and the glaze reach their peak in the firing process at the same time. As the kiln cools, the glaze forms a hard glossy layer on the surface of the pottery.

This second firing completes the process of transforming

your pottery from a fragile substance to one that is rock-hard and water-resistant.

Firing for the correct amount of time and at the correct temperature is crucial, as over- or under-firing a glaze can cause problems. Over-firing can cause the glaze to accumulate at the bottom of a pot, to form blisters or small holes in the surface of the glaze. The holes form when bubbles in the glaze burst as it is being fired. Under-firing can cause pottery to look dull or matte, and give it a rough texture.

SELLING YOUR POTTERY

If making pottery becomes a passion for you, you might start thinking about making it a full-time occupation. You may wonder whether it's possible to make a living from selling pottery, and how to get started.

Once you have gained confidence in your skills and ability to produce pottery that others might want to buy, you need to adopt an optimistic attitude while also remaining realistic. It's unlikely that your pottery will be flying off the shelves right away. You will need to do some networking with other potters and think about how to effectively market your work. Initially your earnings might be low, but these will increase gradually with your experience.

Another way to improve your skills is to connect with a professional potter whose work you admire, and find out whether they would be willing to take on an apprentice. Not only will your skills improve dramatically, but you may also be able to expand your network of connections through a professional potter.

Digital platforms and the rise in popularity of online shopping have revolutionized the options available to artists for selling their work. There are more options for displaying your creations and making them commercially available than ever before. Using digital platforms is by far the best option for small business owners, as it can be done without a great amount of expense, and can reach a very wide audience.

Start by opening a social media account where you can post some pictures of your work, or join a potters' forum where you can gain some constructive criticism and feedback on your work. Look at the work of other potters and note the kind of pieces that they sell. Try to develop an original style, using unique designs or textures that will make your work stand out.

Connect with local art and craft stores that sell handmade items and show them some of your work. Handmade ceramic items are a popular choice for special occasions and holidays like Christmas, Mother's Day, Father's Day, or Valentines Day. These could be a promising first outlet for selling some of your work locally.

You could also approach local coffee shops, furniture stores, and interior designers. Setting up a stall at a flea market or craft fair could also be a great opportunity to market and sell your products.

Then consider creating an eStore and listing your products using Shopify. Make use of a free website-builder like Wordpress or Wix to create a website where you can showcase your work. Or, you could list your products on an existing eCommerce platform or marketplace. Etsy is one such platform that is focused on handmade items, where artists can sell and promote their products. Advertising on social media platforms such as Facebook or Instagram can be used to drive traffic to your website or eCommerce listing. You could even produce custom items through Amazon Custom.

As far as pricing goes, a mug with an unusual or intricate design could be sold for $25- $30. A simple vase could go for around $25, while a larger vase with more complex shapes or decorative techniques can be sold for $80 to $90. Plain serving bowls generally cost around $20 apiece, while larger bowls with more intricate designs can go for $70 or more.

You could eventually turn your studio into a shop, although this depends on the amount of space you have available, and the location and zoning of your home. Ultimately, there are numerous options open to you for making a living from your pottery, if you decide to make it your full-time occupation.

AFTERWORD

Throwing pots on the wheel can seem like an intimidating skill to learn at first. Yet, pottery making is mankind's oldest handicraft, and throwing on the wheel is done in the same way as it was thousands of years ago. While ancient potters would have crafted pottery out of necessity, no doubt they would also have benefited from the calming process of shaping clay. Molding and shaping a natural medium like clay is a grounding practice, and provides a direct connection to the elemental earth.

Starting out requires just a few basic tools and, of course, a pottery wheel for throwing. These are available in a range of different specifications, and you'll need to decide whether to go with an electric or kick wheel pottery wheel. Compare available models for the features they offer, and you're sure to find one that suits your needs and budget.

Choosing the right clay as a beginner is very important; you will want to select a smooth clay that has a decent amount of plasticity. This will allow you to shape it without having to use too much force.

Working with clay offers an infinite number of possibilities, no matter your skill. Once you have a working ability on the wheel, pottery making becomes an absorbing, calming, and therapeutic pastime. The focus required to center your clay and keep it centered as you work, allows you to put all other thoughts aside and enter a state of flow.

This further nourishes your creative process and holds great potential for calming, healing, and transforming your state of mind. Soon you will find that in centering your clay, you become more centered too.

The techniques for wedging clay, centering on the wheel, opening your form, and pulling up the walls are all fundamental to your success as a potter. You will need to use these techniques no matter the kind of forms you want to create. While they may seem challenging at first, you will improve with practice, as you learn the correct positioning of your hands, and the amount of pressure to use.

Learning how to recycle your clay scraps will save you a ton of money on buying new clay. You might even feel inspired to harvest your own clay from your local environment!

Pottery making offers an almost infinite number of possibilities and you will discover that there is always more to learn and explore, and new ideas and forms you will want to try out.

Creating pieces of pottery that you can use in your home or gift to friends and family will leave you with a sense of satisfaction, pride, and accomplishment at what you have achieved. Seeing the results of your efforts, what you have learned and created, will further boost your confidence to try out more challenging forms. You could even start your own pottery business, and sell your work through art shops, markets, or via your own website or eCommerce listing.

Now that you've learned the basic techniques for throwing simple forms on the wheel and the pitfalls to avoid, you can start using these immediately to guide you to success in your pottery-crafting journey.

For more tips and tricks on the potter's wheel for beginners, get connected to my newsletter! Check out my pottery studios on Instagram @muze_arts, or find us on Facebook @Muze Inc.

If you live in the Chicago land area, go to Muzearts.com to book a pottery wheel class with me, or with one of my instructors.

Be on the lookout for my next books on carving, glazing, kilns, studio maintenance, and selling your pottery.

BIBLIOGRAPHY

A mini guide to bisque firing (tips & tricks!). (n.d.). Soul Ceramics. https://www.-soulceramics.com/pages/bisque-firing-guide

Adamant, A. (2018 August 16). *How to process soil into clay for pottery*. Practical Self Reliance. https://practicalselfreliance.com/making-clay/

Allen, J. (n.d.). *A simple handle pulling technique to dress up your pottery*. Ceramic Arts Network. https://ceramicartsnetwork.org/daily/article/A-Simple-Handle-Pulling-Technique-to-Dress-Up-Your- Pottery

Beginner's guide to throwing a bowl. (2017 December 22). Earth Nation Ceramics. https://www.youtube.com/watch?v=Nzq2Yd7mlsk

Best pottery wheels: in-depth buying guide for beginners. (2021 October 20). The Beginning Artist. https://www.thebeginningartist.com/best-pottery-wheels/

Bottle & jugs—part 1. (2016 October 6). Corvallis Schools Art Department. https://www.youtube.com/watch?v=e0LcvX6u9KU

Burris, C. (n.d.-a). *Beginning ceramics: how to throw a bottle*. https://www.youtube.com/watch?v=AT4kpYLbOqU

Burris, C. (n.d.-b). *Beginning ceramics: How to throw a bowl*. https://www.youtube.com/watch?v=0bKRJ8-gMr0

Centering for beginners. (2017 October 13). ClayCraft. https://www.claycraft.co.uk/how-to/centering-for-beginners/

Ceramics, K. (2017 August 5). *Throwing mug forms*. https://www.youtube.com/watch?v=WQXziyZ4NCM

Cipala, A. (2022 January 7). *6 Great Tips for Carving Pottery*. Ceramic Arts Network. https://ceramicartsnetwork.org/daily/article/6-Great-Tips-for-Carving-Pottery

Clay forming techniques. (n.d.). Clay Times Magazine. http://www.claytimes.com/reference-guide/forming-techniques.html

Clay, T. (2013 March 16). *Help! I hate trimming*. Www.youtube.com. https://www.youtube.com/watch?v=HCRqtvwRVrA

Coldiron, R. (2021 April 23). *Want to start making your own pottery? These are the essential tools and materials you'll need*. Martha Stewart. https://www.-marthastewart.com/8094778/best-pottery-tools-materials

D'Souza, S. (2018 September 11). *How to bisque or biscuit fire pottery*. The Spruce Crafts. https://www.thesprucecrafts.com/how-to-bisque-fire-pottery-2745874

Doyle, C. L. (2017). Creative flow as a unique cognitive process. *Frontiers in Psychology*, 8. https://doi.org/10.3389/fpsyg.2017.01348

Earth Nation Ceramics. (n.d.). *Collaring and choking for beginners*. https://www.youtube.com/watch?v=umtwyBcYhiE

Earth Nation Ceramics. (2018a). *Beginners guide to throwing a plate on the Wheel*. https://www.youtube.com/watch?v=ndtvTw2SZYM

Earth Nation Ceramics. (2018b August 24). *How to make a gallery lid jar*. https://www.youtube.com/watch?app=desktop&feature=sh+are&v=7B_GljX52w8

Earth Nation Ceramics. (2019a February 8). *Beginners guide to making a functional teapot*. Www.youtube.com. https://www.youtube.com/watch?v=f2HrBjd4kQk

Earth Nation Ceramics. (2019b May 10). *Pulling for beginners (common mistakes)*. Www.youtube.com. https://www.youtube.com/watch?v=psiJ7QaqnbE

Field, A. (2022, April 11). *Tips for throwing a perfect tall cylinder*. Ceramic Arts Network. https://ceramicartsnetwork.org/daily/article/Tips-for-Throwing-a-Perfect-Tall-Cylinder

Gadsby, F. (n.d.-a). *How I reclaim, cut wedge and spiral wedge my clay*. Www.youtube.com. https://www.youtube.com/watch?v=mco55yi_U6s

Gadsby, F. (n.d.-b). *How to throw and trim a bowl*. Www.youtube.com. https://www.youtube.com/watch?v=zYg3UZEHAwc

Gadsby, F. (n.d.-c). *How to throw and trim a small pottery plate*. Www.youtube.com. https://www.youtube.com/watch?v=AFeR_Ns9oBc

Hansen-Gard, J. (2021 November 25). *How to wedge clay properly*. Ceramic Arts Network. https://ceramicartsnetwork.org/daily/article/How-to-Wedge-Clay-Properly

Hopper, R. (2011 September 23). *Centering, throwing and trimming tips from an expert Potter*. Ceramic Arts Network. https://ceramicartsnetwork.org/daily/article/Centering-Throwing-and-Trimming-Tips-From-an-Expert-Potter

How To Buy The Right Pottery Wheel—6 key considerations. (n.d.). Soul Ceramics. https://www.soulceramics.com/pages/what-to-look-for-when-buying-a-pottery-wheel#

How to clean your studio for a safe working environment. (2017 September 20). The Ceramic School. https://ceramic.school/how-to-clean-your-studio/

How to make a one piece lidded jar. (2017 August 28). The Ceramic School. https://ceramic.school/make-one-piece-lidded-jar/

How to make a plaster slab for wedging and recycling clay (easy). (2021 February 12). Www.youtube.com; Earth Nation Ceramics. https://www.youtube.-com/watch?v=ZciM2V6dudQ

How to pull a handle. (n.d.). Instructables. https://www.instructables.-com/How-to-pull-a-handle/

How to select the right clay body for a studio or classroom? (n.d.). Www.lakeside-pottery.com. https://www.lakesidepottery.com/Pages/Pottery-tips/choos-ing-the-right-clay-type.htm

Hughes, J. (2010 April 14). *Pottery—how to center clay on the wheel*. Www.y-outube.com; Evolution Stoneware. https://www.youtube.com/watch?v=seZbyX1gpyc

Ingleton Pottery. (n.d.). *Throwing/making a pottery teapot on the wheel*. Www.y-outube.com. https://www.youtube.com/watch?v=syVvZtD2Dcg

Jabbur, M. (n.d.). *Tips and tools: trimming with a chuck*. Ceramic Arts Network. https://ceramicartsnetwork.org/ceramics-monthly/ceramics-monthly-article/Tips-and-Tools-Trimming-with-a- Chuck#

Karans Pots And Glass. (2014). *Throwing a plate on the potter's wheel*. Www.y-outube.com. https://www.youtube.com/watch?v=QSRQUwCuj-w

Karans Pots and Glass. (2020 March 18). *Making a pitcher with a pulled handle on the potter's wheel*. Www.youtube.com. https://www.youtube.com/watch?v=CVOqGrrFZzc

Kotler, S. (2014). Flow states and creativity. *Psychology Today*. https://www.psychologytoday.com/us/blog/the-playing-field/201402/flow-states-and-creativity

Kvarnstrom, E. (2015 December 7). *The shape of healing: the power of pottery in mental health treatment*. Bridges to Recovery. https://www.bridgestorecov-ery.com/blog/the-shape-of-healing-the-power-of-pottery-in-mental-health-treatment/

Lark Crafts. (n.d.). *Ceramics for beginners: wheel throwing—trimming a bowl with*

Emily Reason. Www.youtube.com. https://www.youtube.com/watch?v=xuOXD8A10aw&t=75s

Lesley. (2020a January 31). *Choosing a pottery glaze—a beginners guide to ceramic glazes.* Pottery Tips by the Pottery Wheel. https://thepotterywheel.com/choosing-a-pottery-glaze/

Lesley. (2020b July 28). *Types of clay for pottery—the 5 main types of ceramic clay.* Pottery Tips by the Pottery Wheel. https://thepotterywheel.com/types-of-clay-for-pottery/#ball

Lesley. (2021a January 26). *What is glaze firing?—all about glaze firing pottery.* Pottery Tips by the Pottery Wheel. https://thepotterywheel.com/what-is-glaze-firing/

Lesley. (2021b September 27). *S cracks in pottery—what causes them & how to prevent them.* Pottery Tips by the Pottery Wheel. https://thepotterywheel.com/s-cracks-in-pottery/

Lin, H. (2010 October 12). 25. *Throwing / making mugs & pulling / attaching handles with Hsin-Chuen Lin* 林新春 馬克杯拉坯修坯接把示範. Www.youtube.com. https://www.youtube.com/watch?v=ZZSTxUNoy_o

Little Street Pottery. (n.d.-a). *5 mistakes to avoid when shaping mugs—how to fix them!* Www.youtube.com. https://www.youtube.com/watch?v=lxD6It0FB1Y

Little Street Pottery. (n.d.-b). *7 simple and stunning handles for pottery!* Www.youtube.com. https://www.youtube.com/watch?v=U7p8Lvm1k1M

Little Street Pottery. (n.d.-c). *How to make great lids for your pottery—throwing lids and pots.* Www.youtube.com. https://www.youtube.com/watch?v=-fH6BNWJ9gY

Little Street Pottery. (n.d.-d). *How to trim pottery—easy and fun way to learn trimming techniques.* Www.youtube.com. https://www.youtube.com/watch?v=7TJSr2w8Ubs

Magyar, C. (2020 May 26). *How to harvest clay for pottery & natural building.* Rural Sprout. https://www.ruralsprout.com/harvest-clay/

Mansur, R. (2010 March 3). *How to collar ceramics.* WonderHowTo. https://ceramics.wonderhowto.com/how-to/collar-ceramics-241897/

Marie. (2019 March 23). *Choosing your pottery clay—best pottery clay for beginners.* Pottery Crafters. https://potterycrafters.com/best-pottery-clay-for-beginners/

Marie. (2020a June 21). *What Are the four types of clay?* Pottery Crafters.

https://potterycrafters.com/what-are-the-four-types-of-clay/

Marie. (2020b September 28). *How to make a living selling pottery: a step-by-step guide.* Pottery Crafters. https://potterycrafters.com/how-to-make-a-living-selling-pottery/

Marie. (2020c October 18). *How to glaze pottery—9 pottery glazing techniques.* Pottery Crafters. https://potterycrafters.com/how-to-glaze-pottery-9-pottery-glazing-techniques/

Marie. (2021a September 17). *Which direction should a potter's wheel turn?* Pottery Crafters. https://potterycrafters.com/which-direction-should-a-potters-wheel-turn/

Marie. (2021b November 5). *11 problems centering clay and easy ways to fix them.* Pottery Crafters. https://potterycrafters.com/11-problems-centering-clay-and-easy-ways-to-fix-them/

Marie. (2021c November 5). *What is slip trailing? Glazing tips, tools, and ideas.* Pottery Crafters. https://potterycrafters.com/what-is-slip-trailing/

Marie. (2021d November 6). *Pottery wheels reviewed.* Pottery Crafters. https://potterycrafters.com/pottery-wheels-reviewed/

Marie. (2022 March 4). *Pottery clay dust—how to minimize it.* Pottery Crafters. https://potterycrafters.com/pottery-clay-dust-how-to-minimize-it/

Munn, J. (2021 October 27). *Slip trailing for beginners: An introduction to the slip trailing technique.* Ceramic Arts Network. https://ceramicartsnetwork.org/daily/article/Slip-Trailing-for-Beginners-A-Primer-on-a-Great-Ceramics-Decorating-Technique

Petersen, B. (2019a). *A quick guide to basic pottery tools.* The Spruce Crafts. https://www.thesprucecrafts.com/survey-of-basic-pottery-tools-2746328

Petersen, B. (2019b). *Is there a difference between pottery and ceramics?* The Spruce Crafts. https://www.thesprucecrafts.com/what-are-pottery-and-ceramics-2745954

Petersen, B. (2019c October 21). *What is grog in pottery?* The Spruce Crafts. https://www.thesprucecrafts.com/grog-2746004

Petersen, B. (2019d October 23). *What is leather-hard pottery?* The Spruce Crafts. https://www.thesprucecrafts.com/leather-hard-2746007

Petersen, B. (2020a January 13). *Why you should start creating pottery with clay.* The Spruce Crafts. https://www.thesprucecrafts.com/start-out-with-clay-2746271

Petersen, B. (2020b January 18). *How to make handles for pottery.* The Spruce

Crafts. https://www.thesprucecrafts.com/how-to-make-handles-for-pottery-2745736

Petersen, B. (2020c April 8). *How to find or create a small pottery studio*. The Spruce Crafts. https://www.thesprucecrafts.com/set-up-your-pottery-studio-2746268

Petersen, B. (2020d May 19). *How to center clay on the potter's wheel*. The Spruce Crafts. https://www.thesprucecrafts.com/how-to-center-clay-potters-wheel-2745815

Petersen, B. (2020e July 8). *How to recycle clay scraps into workable clay*. The Spruce Crafts. https://www.thesprucecrafts.com/how-to-recycle-clay-scraps-2745848

Pottery Crafters. (2020 July 30). *How to make colored slip easy with no lumps*. Www.youtube.com. https://www.youtube.com/watch?v=95KkiwlOOko

Queen City Clay. (2020 April 7). *Collaring, the claw, and fire*. Www.youtube.com. https://www.youtube.com/watch?v=Kur-VHMMLIY

Rhee, M. (n.d.). *Tips and tools: reclaiming clay*. Ceramic Arts Network. https://ceramicartsnetwork.org/ceramics-monthly/ceramics-monthly-article/Tips-and-Tools-Reclaiming-Clay-202916#

Robb, A. (2019). *The "flow state": Where creative work thrives*. BBC.com. https://www.bbc.com/worklife/article/20190204-how-to-find-your-flow-state-to-be-peak-creative

Shears, E. (2021 November 7). *How to center clay on the wheel like a pro*. Artabys. https://artabys.com/how-to-center-clay-on-the-wheel-like-a-pro/

Throwing a basic Pot. Pottery wheel step-by-step tutorial. (n.d.). Www.lakeside-pottery.com. https://www.lakesidepottery.com/Pages/Pottery-tips/Throwing-a-pot-Lakeside-Pottery-Tutorial.htm

Top 10 health benefits of pottery. (2017 March 17). ClayGround Studio & Gallery. https://claygroundonline.com/health-benefits-of-pottery/

van Gilder, B. (2011 August 19). *Great tips for throwing great plates on the pottery wheel*. Ceramic Arts Network. https://ceramicartsnetwork.org/daily/article/Great-Tips-for-Throwing-Great-Plates-on-the-Pottery-Wheel

Vito, D. (n.d.). *Making better pots*. Fireborn. https://fireborn.com/become-a-better-potter/

Walther, J. (2022,April 26). *How to throw a well functioning pitcher on the pottery wheel*. Ceramic Arts Network. https://ceramicartsnetwork.org/daily/article/How-to-Throw-a-Well-Functioning-Pitcher-on-the-Pottery-Wheel

Wedging boards—all you need to know. (2017 June 20). The Ceramic School. https://ceramic.school/wedging-boards/

What is ball clay? (n.d.). Www.clayheritage.org. http://www.clayheritage.org/introduction-to-the-ball-clays-of-devon-and-dorset/what-is-ball-clay

What is Sgraffito? Pottery history, technique .& designs. (2021 September 1). Crafts Hero. https://craftshero.com/sgraffito-pottery/

What is Sgraffito? Pottery Technique and Tools. (n.d.). Lakesidepottery.com. https://lakesidepottery.com/Pages/Pottery-tips/How-to-create-sgraffito-pottery-tutorial.htm

Woodrow, J. (2022 May 25). *Relief carving techniques for expressive functional pottery.* Ceramic Arts Network. https://ceramicartsnetwork.org/daily/article/Relief-Carving-Techniques-for-Expressive-Functional-Pottery

Made in United States
North Haven, CT
02 November 2024

59602591R10117